I'VE BEEN IN SCOTLAND
AFORE YE

... I should not paint the moon faithfully, if I
marked not her spots.

JAMES KIRKTON: *History of the Church of Scotland (1620-1699)*

I've been in Scotland Afore Ye

A Scots-American looks at
Scotland & the Scots

JEANNIE SHARP

CHARLES SKILTON
The Albyn Press
EDINBURGH

© 1973 Eugenia Callander Sharp

Published by
THE ALBYN PRESS
3 Abbeymount
Edinburgh
and
50 Alexandra Road
London SW19

Printed in Scotland by
Robert Maclehose & Co. Ltd.,
Glasgow

 **LONDON BOROUGH OF LEWISHAM**

LIBRARY SERVICE

Author _____

Title _____

Books or discs must be returned on or before the last date stamped on label or on card in book pocket. Books or discs can be renewed by telephone, letter or personal call unless required by another reader. After library hours use the Ansafone Service (01-698 7347). For hours of opening and charges see notices at the above branch, but note that all lending departments close at 1 pm on Wednesday and all libraries are closed on Sundays, Good Friday, Christmas Day, Bank Holidays and Saturdays prior to Bank Holidays.

Contents

Contents

For Freddie
For Scotland
for friends 'aye'

1. O, Caledonia!

SCOTLAND – seemingly forever the stranger. How does one get to know this land? Well, it takes time. A very long time. But then, everything in Scotland takes a long time. After all, it takes twelve years to create an acceptable whisky, seven years and seven generations to make a piper, three centuries to grow that deep, thick, green velvet carpet the Scots refer to casually as 'grass', and a full hour for the hotel floor maid to bring you your morning tea or coffee from the pantry three doors along the corridor. Yes, it is possible to make friends with Scotland. All you need is patience.

Getting acquainted with Scotland is like finding oneself in the same city with a distant maiden cousin. If you have any love of family, you feel that you really ought to meet her. You've heard that she is a bit eccentric, but you decide to give it a go and arrange to pay a call. She is a relative and, perhaps, she is not as strange as you have been led to believe. But your worst suspicions are confirmed when you enter the gloomy fortress of her spinsterhood. She's friendly enough, but obviously she's quite potty. Isn't she? Or is she? Or is it *you* who are out of balance? You wonder and ponder and, later on, you pay another call and yet another. And in the end, you rather get to love the old girl. You become devoted, even. But again, it does take time and it may or may not be worth the effort. That depends entirely on *you* and on your attitudes.

2. The High Road

THE BEST way to approach Scotland is direct by air to Prestwick, unsullied by the touch of Rome or Paris. Come prepared for an exciting experience to be remembered all of your life, to be cherished, to be returned to again and again.

Of course, if the jet is not for you, come by ship to Greenock, but Clydeside being what it is, the effect is not quite the same.

Freddie and I have found that the best transatlantic route is by night flight. You leave the sunset behind and soar up into a deep magical darkness. If you are fortunate, the moon will be shining on the wing. And then, in about four hours, you witness the first miracle that is Scotland. It is a simple, mundane occurrence. The sun rises! But it rises on an Old World that seems as new and pristine as it was on the day of creation. First, a streak of pearl pink. Then a ruby glow. Very soon, the plane's cabin glows with something like the promise of childhood re-visited. If your luck still holds, since it rains more than is really necessary on the west coast, the captain will announce that the skies are clear at Prestwick and the ground temperature is somewhere between forty and fifty degrees, if your arrival is in the summer, or between thirty and forty degrees, if in winter. He would feel he was going too far were he to tell the truth and report that the air is as sweet as milk. It would destroy the confidence of the passengers who want a space scientist at the controls, not a poet.

Now, it is light enough to look down and see something. And there they are – The Islands. Mull, Colonsay, Jura, Islay. At the moment, they'll mean nothing to you. Just names. In fact you can't tell one from the other. Never mind – few people can from that altitude. But someday those names of Mull, Colonsay, Jura and Islay will hold a special magic of their own.

Your plane flies in low. To your right is Arran and the peak of Goatfell rises high, a mountain terribly smug in its majesty, too large for such a small island. Then comes a short wave-skimming rush across the waters of the Firth of Clyde and you swoop straight on in and touch down, rolling, rolling past what appears to be an interminable line of chicken coops. You have arrived!

3. For Auld Lang Syne, My Jo

I MUST keep reminding myself that this is not really a travel book in the truest sense. These are impressions, intensely personal. And more: I have a great love which I want to share with others because my devotion to the home of my forefathers is deep and broad and abiding.

Returning briefly to the flight to Scotland: I do hope you are able to travel with a group of homeward bound Scots, men and women who have been away, some perhaps for as long as forty years. Seating on a plane is a game of roulette, but if you should find yourself, by chance, seated near some of these expatriates, listen to them closely.

At first, you will hear mild banter with the stewardesses. Then, as these Scots discover each other, the conversation becomes more intense. After their second whisky and a Guinness with dinner, you may find that you have lost the thread of their conversation. But no matter. Just understand that you are hearing the voice of Scotland – not Highland nor Lowland. That comes later. There is a spirit and a strength behind these people who are encased and decompressed with you. These are the men and women who uprooted the hardihood, the optimism, the realistic good humour and the intelligence of their tribe and planted it in the New World. Not all of them have made fortunes. They are not necessarily going home rich. The Scots have all of the riches necessary for any human being. They are simply returning home, joyfully, respectfully, to what they left behind. It may be a croft in the bleak hills of Ross and Cromarty, a stone cottage in a fisherman's village in the Kingdom of Fife, a tall tenement in the Gorbals of Glasgow, a flat above an ironmonger's shop in Ayrshire. It makes no difference to them. They are going home. All they ask is that the croft, the cottage, the tenement, the flat and all who abide therein are the same as when they left. The Scots deeply resent change. After all, your fellow passengers may have cherished their memories for ten, twenty, forty years.

As they near the coast, the old, antic feud breaks out, a bit ribald, caustic, a blunted, verbal dirk point: Highlander against Lowlander. Scots aye, flinty Highlander strikes hard against the softer Lowlander who learned to accommodate. 'Slainte Gael' against 'Scotland Forever!' It means the same thing, really.

As the plane crosses the islands, noses press against the windows, necks crane for a 'keek' at the dearly beloved, eyes mist over, silence follows. But not for long. This is not the nature of the Scot. A homely excitement begins to bubble and boil.

'This efternuin I'll walk aaal th' way hame frae Wemyss along th' shore.'

B

'Just wait ye 'til MacRae sees me walk into th' Kings Arms th' nicht!'

'I wonder, Hamish, are th' salmon runnin' by th' Brig doon t' Ballantrae. I'd like it fine tae gang alang doon this evin and gie a look.'

This afternoon, tonight, this evening! Never tomorrow. Today. Now is the time of the heart and the things the heart has remembered for so many years. Today. They're home at last. Home, until they feel they must leave again, some never to return.

4. *Half A Loaf Is Better Than None*

IF YOU are a collector of European cities (21-day excursion, jet economy class, best hotels, room with bath, modified American plan, all gratuities, experienced tour guides, London, Edinburgh, Paris, Geneva, Vienna, Rome and Madrid), then forget about Edinburgh. It's not for you. Don't come to Edinburgh for one or two days and, then, say you've 'Done Scotland'. You haven't. You haven't even 'Done Edinburgh'. It takes three days even to begin to 'feel' Edinburgh.

But, if you *must* (and who am I to try to stop you) spend a day panting up the Royal Mile, take your coach tour of the Trossachs, clamber off of the bus to stand on a hill by Loch Katrine and listen with completely un-merited reverence to a lone and rather tatty piper who doesn't know a true grace note from his big toe; and then, spend your travellers' cheques in craftsy, tweedy little shops with tartan carpets in that lamentable tourist trap called Callander. (May my grandfather – a Callander of that Ilk – forgive me!)

Back in your hotel, put on your newly-purchased Tam O'Shanter or Victorian Glengarry bonnet, the tie and vest in a tartan that undoubtedly has no connection with your family (especially since the tourists' favourites are the Royal Stuart or the mighty and glorious Black Watch) and preen to your heart's content. But, please, don't wear them beyond the door to your room. And above all, don't let your wife buy a sporran for a 'ducky little over-the-shoulder purse'. Thanks be to St Andrew, the gentleman's kilt and proper jacket, Balmoral bonnet, crest pin, kilt hose, flashes, skean dhu, leather sporran and brogues are beyond the wallet of the average 'capital collector'.

Should you desire a fitting memento, buy your wife a cairngorm-set, thistle brooch and get for yourself a Highland industry mohair shawl, just the ticket for a winter Sunday nap.

5. Scotland Forever!

SCOTLAND, contrary to the belief of some 'capital collectors', is *not* the northern part of England. Historically, morally, socially and psychologically, Scotland is a country rampant on her own two feet, the Act of Union to the contrary. Scotland's first sovereign was Malcolm II, whose reign united the country's component parts in 1005, and her last was James VI, who by a fluke of birth also took on the Throne of England. Not that he shied away from the proposition. It has been noted, even, that he winked at what was tantamount to matricide in order to wear both crowns. But don't ever let those south of the border tell you that James was an English king. He was a Scot who became king of England. James died in 1625 and from that time on England and Scotland had one king or one queen or one dictator (Cromwell) as the case may have been at the moment, and all went reasonably well, for *those* times at least, until politics and religion became just too sticky a wicket to be resolved and the Stuarts were ousted in favor of a remote Hanoverian relative – 'the wee, wee German Lairdie' – who spoke neither English, nor good Scots, let alone did he have the Gaelic. As the old Jacobite song went, 'But the very dogs of England's court, they bark and howl in German.'

The last two Stuarts, the legitimate heirs to the double throne, the Old Pretender, James VIII of Scotland (III of England) and his son, Bonnie Prince Charlie, the Young Pretender, made two romantic, abortive attempts at regaining the sovereignty to which James, alas a Roman Catholic, had the true and dynastic right. And that was the end of it. Historically, Scotland lost her rightful king, the 'guidman' of the Jacobites, and died as a nation in agony and treachery on a bleak day in April on the misty battlefield of Culloden in the year 1746. *Sic transit gloria jacobus.* The 'hero' of that disgraceful day was William, Duke of Cumberland, com-

monly known as 'Butcher'. In England, they named a flower for
him, 'Sweet William'. In Scotland, it is considered to be a weed,
called 'Stinky Willie'.

For whatever it may be worth, between 1054 and 1746, Scottish
soldiers fought forty-seven major battles, a shocking percentage
of them over the simple fact that Scotland was a sovereign nation,
a point hard to make with the English, who kept at the fray with
bull-dog intensity until they finally triumphed. I have, perhaps,
over-simplified, but I doubt that the English would have won if
the Scots had not been their own worst enemies. Not all Scots were
loyal to the Cause. The situation has an Alice-in-Wonderland
quality, quite unbelievable. There are many ugly facets to the
mirror of the time: clan warfare, jealousy, an overwhelming
desire for power derived from Royal Favour, and religion – the
Roman Catholicism of the Highlands and the Calvinism of the
Lowlands. If the Scots had all been loyal to their Cause, history
might have told a quite different story.

Don't misunderstand. Jacobite to the very core, I revere Her
Majesty. Tears come to my eyes when God is implored to save the
Queen. But I love and respect her, first, because she is a marvellous woman; and, second and most important, because she is half-
Scottish. Therefore, seated on her double throne, Elizabeth is a
true representative of the land of her Scots mother. Perhaps
there is in this a certain poetic justice. The Scots truly love their
countrywoman, Queen Elizabeth, the Queen Mother, and I feel
that the same love for her daughter was best expressed by an
ancient Highlander who caused a delighted smile to break out on
the young queen's face when he spoke to her in Gaelic and called
his monarch 'mo chaileag', 'my lassie'.

6. The Nobil Toun

BOOKS by the score have been written about Edinburgh. Many of
them (especially the most recent) are excellent, and the visitor
who wishes to spend some time in this fascinating city would do
well to read one of them in advance of a visit. Apparently, a great
many men have had a love affair with Edinburgh and it would be
next to impossible to write a dull book about such a city.

Countryside, landscape, can stand on its own, lovely, awesome or just plain dreary. God made it – there it is, and make of it what you will. But a city, now that's a different story. Man makes a city and it is a personality to be studied, especially an old city where every cobbled street corner was a witness to history, where tragedy or triumph was enacted in this old house or that. You can love or despise a city, like a person, but you must study it in all of its complexities before you know what you are talking about.

If schizophrenic can be made to sound like a compliment, a desirable personality trait, then that is exactly what Edinburgh is. In fact, if Edinburgh weren't split, the entire personality of the city would be lost. And split it is, physically, like a great grey trout laid wide open on a platter. One half is medieval, the other half Georgian, and right down the middle runs the stiff, unbending backbone that is uncompromisingly Victorian.

The medieval side, the Old Town, whose origins lie in the murk of history, plays Mr Hyde to the Dr Jekyll of the other side, the scientific, precise New Town. I hope – I *believe*, rather – that Robert Louis Stevenson will understand this character reversal. While Henry Jekyll created the evil Hyde of himself, by his own doing, it was the Old Town, the scene of dark and cruel deeds, that created the New Town. The meaning of this may be elusive to you at the moment, but once you've walked about Edinburgh through wide streets and narrow, preferably in a misty gloom after tea, you will most likely see, or better still feel, exactly what I mean.

The middle, the backbone, the Victoriana, is the Princes Street Gardens. This gully, once a boggy lake, called Nor' Loch, was filled in and now a garden, plus some railway tracks better left undiscussed, cover the ground between the sheer cliff of the Old Town and the shopper's heaven, Princes Street. This strip, nearly a mile long, is Victorian because that was when it was embellished, or *over*-embellished; and one look at the North British Hotel, the Royal Scottish Academy, the National Gallery, the Scott Monument, the Floral Clock, the Bandstand and, about half-way up the hill, the Bank of Scotland, is all that is needed to savour the full flavour of unadulterated Victoriana. But, in its own way, this is all very fitting. Tourism in Scotland owes a great debt both to Queen Victoria and to Sir Walter Scott. They made Scotland, Highlands and Lowlands, popular in Great Britain and throughout the world. Victoria travelled extensively in Scotland during her reign and it was she who wrote in her later published journal, 'Every year my heart becomes more fixed in this dear paradise.' As to Sir Walter, he wrote copiously, novel after novel, poem after poem, rather unfortunately romanticizing the darker deeds of Scottish history; but everyone read them and millions still do. Who cannot feel a tug at the old heart strings when one reads:

> Harp of the North, farewell! The Hills grow dark,
>   On purple peaks a deeper shade descending;
> In twilight copse the glow-worm lights her spark,
>   The deer, half-seen, are to the covert wending.

Or from 'Marmion':

> Such dusky grandeur clothed the height,
> Where the huge castle holds its state,
> And all the steep slope down,
> Whose ridgy back heaves to the sky,
> Piled deep and massy, close and high
> Mine own romantic town!

In some respects, 'Auld Reekie' is quite unchanged since the days of Queen Victoria and Scott. It's become a little 'aulder', but happily it's not as 'reekie' since bans have been put on smoking chimney pots. 'Lang may your lum reek' was once a wish for a successful future of full and plenty from one friend to another; but now the city fathers have begun looking askance at those thousands of lums poking skywards and have officially, but politely, suggested that they reek no more.

A second, and terribly important, factor in the character of Edinburgh is weather. We must face up to facts right away, without flinching from the truth, no matter how coldly implacable. It does rain in Scotland. It's not the wettest spot in the world, though. That honour is reserved, believe it or not, for Mount Waialeale in Hawaii, and that's a tropic paradise, which Scotland definitely is not. I'm not about to gloss over the fact of rain in rather copious amounts by saying, 'It's good for the lawns. See how green everything is!' The visitor couldn't care less. He's only there for a brief spell of sightseeing and, besides, it's not *his* lawn that's gaining the benefit. Rain in the country, while not always passionately desirable, is more natural and bearable, but rain in the city can be a bit of a pain in the neck. If one hits a run of rainy weather in Edinburgh, one is apt to mope about the hotel the first day. On the second, a planned trip to Loch Lomond will be put off 'until tomorrow when the sun is shining'. An awfully good idea, that: Loch Lomond in the rain is very, very drear. On the third day, all optimism having been blasted, one is tempted to shout something dim-witted like, 'For goodness sake, turn off the shower. You're wasting water.'

This is all wrong. In Edinburgh, rain can be turned to an advantage. In fact, Edinburgh has very strange weather all the way round, but it is part and parcel of the city, and, if you don't fight it, the weather can make your visit memorable in more ways than one.

I have mentioned rain. That's just one item on the weather agenda. There's also the 'haar', a rather cold mist that blows in off of the North Sea and envelopes the city like a shroud. Then, there's a heat wave. Believe me, I am perfectly serious when I say that when the sun is shining (it really does) and the temperature shoots up to 73 degrees, you will feel as though you have fallen headlong into a blast furnace. You'll find yourself creeping along the shady side of the streets and staring in disbelief at old 'wifies' all done up in tweed coats and winter woollies, stumping along as determinedly as through a blizzard. The trick is to emulate the Scots. Don't pay any attention to the weather. Ignore its caprices completely. Life does go on. So be about your business of enjoying the city according to the mood that *it*, not you, happens to be in.

For instance, take rain. You've got to. There's no other choice. Now, what can you do on a rainy day? Quite a number of things, depending on your interests. First, there's the Castle. Even if you've already been up there once, that's no excuse for not going up again. There's so much to see after you've done a guided tour. For the historian, the military enthusiast or the merely intellectually curious, I suggest that you go directly to the Scottish United Services Museum or to the Scottish National War Memorial. Take your time. See it all, slowly. No one will push you along. This, I know from experience, is a grand thing to do on a rainy morning.

Art lovers can stroll happily through the National Gallery of Scotland and the Royal Scottish Academy. Both of these are conveniently located on the Mound at Princes Street. A few blocks away, up on Queen Street in the New Town, is the Scottish National Portrait Gallery. From here you can dash between the raindrops to the Cafe Royal, one of the more interesting of Edinburgh's old restaurants, for a very good luncheon. If it should be tea-time, try the George Hotel, also nearby.

Those who are *addicted* to museums in general would find much of interest in the Royal Scottish Museum, out near the university.

If there is shopping you wish to do, you can do that. But window-shopping would best be put off until another day.

Now, if none of this appeals, you can always sulk in the American bar of your hotel, but that does seem a coward's way out and not particularly inventive.

The heat wave, which I assure you will be of short duration, can be sat-out under the trees in the Princes Street Gardens. There's generally an 'event' going on in summer, a band concert or a dance exhibition, and you may take your ease on one of the many benches scattered throughout the Gardens, each marked with a plaque, 'Gifted by ——'.

As to the 'haar', this affords a unique chance to go up to the Castle and see the mist swirling around the ancient battlements. The twentieth century will fade into the distance and you will be drawn three or four centuries back into history and you'll find your ears straining for the sound of soldiers' clattering, running feet and the sound of the pipes calling them to the Castle's defence.

Now that we've taken care of the more extreme examples of Edinburgh's weather and what to do about them, let us assume that you have arrived for your visit during a spell of perfectly normal Scottish weather: bright, cool days or light, intermittent rain. You have checked into your hotel and unpacked as much as you care to and you're ready to start on your tour of the city. First, put on comfortable shoes. Edinburgh is a city where you walk a great deal and in some sections sidewalks are rather haphazard. You can't enjoy yourself if your feet hurt. Then, put on a raincoat. You simply never know when you will need it. Besides, it seems to provide just the right amount of warmth when walking or being in and out of buildings. When you're going sightseeing, I suggest that the ladies take a small handbag. Those great travelling handbags, while perfect for beating the airline's forty-four pound limit, weigh like a ton of bricks after a few hours and are just about as useful. In the bag all you really need is some money (especially a supply of coins), a credit card or travellers' cheques, and a few of those pre-moistened towelettes. If you've ever examined a public wash-room roller towel, you'll never travel without them. Now, unless your friends are all doubting Thomases, your nearest and dearest will know that you have gone to Europe and there is really no reason to go about your sightseeing with the one idea in mind of taking pictures to show 'the folks back home'. It is such a ridiculous waste of time, money and energy. There you go with your cameras and light-meters and carrying cases slung like albatrosses around your necks, worrying about light and perspective and focus and who moved just as the picture was being taken. Do you really have to prove you were there? If the answer is negative and all you want are pictures to look at next winter, then let me remind you that you can buy fine slide sets of practically everything worth seeing, taken by professional photographers who can afford to wait around for just the right light. And, if you keep your mouth shut, who's going to know you didn't take them yourself?

Since Edinburgh is so neatly divided geographically, you can just as neatly divide up your sightseeing so that you will have a clear-cut memory to take home with you instead of the haphazard jumble which sightseeing in some cities becomes. The word 'sightseeing' when applied to Edinburgh is rather a misnomer. You don't have to sprint from pillar to post to see the sights, miles apart from each other. In Edinburgh, it's the whole city you want to see, to absorb. The city is the 'sight' in itself.

The natural place to start is in the Old Town. No one will dispute that fact. But what I do find absurd are the far too many guidebooks that refer to going *up* the Royal Mile. It's a stiffish climb and I can't imagine why anyone would recommend it. So we shall do the unconventional, but natural, thing and go *down*.

We begin by taking a taxi, one of those glorious British taxis, and drive in state up to the Castle Esplanade. There you alight and, if it is a decent day (in other words if you can see beyond the ramparts or as far as Princes Street on one side and Johnston Terrace on the other) wander about for awhile looking out over the city and admire the facade of the Castle. The Esplanade is noted for three things. Here, executions by axe took place, the Tattoo of the Edinburgh Festival is held each year, and lastly, it is legally part of Canadian Nova Scotia. This is a fact not too well known, even by Scots, and you might find it of interest to discover why, which is too long and involved to go into here except to say that in order to finance the development of Nova Scotia in 1624, money was raised for the project by promising baronies in Nova Scotia to the donors. In order to save the Nova Scotia barons an arduous trip to the New World, the oath was taken on the Castle Esplanade which was declared, for the sake of the ceremony, to be part of Nova Scotia.

For your first visit to the Castle, may I suggest that you purchase a guide book and join, for a small fee, a group clustered about a commissionaire who will give you a thorough and knowledgeable tour from inside the main gate and guard house until he leaves you in front of the National War Memorial. During that corkscrewing trip, as you climb higher and higher, he will have pointed out with appropriate and often amusing remarks the old state prison or Argyll's Tower, several batteries with breathtaking views out over the city and countryside, Mons Meg and St Margaret's Chapel. At each of these are spectacular views, as you might well imagine, since the summit of Castle Hill is 433 feet above sea level. At the top of the rock are the Royal Apartments and the Great Hall. The Royal Apartments are hardly luxurious but for some odd reason you feel very close to Mary, Queen of Scots. This beautiful, but misguided, young queen lived in many palaces in her realm, but here in the room where she gave birth to her son James VI, she steps out of the pages of history and becomes a human being. If you can find yourself alone in her private apartments – and this often happens – and if you have any feeling for her, you can almost hear her breathing beside you. This is the one place where I sense the spirit of Mary. I feel that she will always live on here and if she ever does return in the small hours of the morning this is the place where she would come.

The Great Hall is magnificent, and it is fun for the imaginative to re-create the banquets and balls that took place here. For many, many years, balls have been given in the Edinburgh Assembly Rooms and in the Royal Chapel (long since de-consecrated) at Stirling Castle; but it is in the Great Hall at Edinburgh Castle where I often dream of treading the stately measures of a strathspey.

The Honours of Scotland – such a lovely title – the State Crown, the Sceptre and the great Sword of State, both the gifts of Popes, after a long and adventurous history of theft, of being hidden, lost and recovered, are on safe display in the Castle and well worth a visit. So seldom are they used that they seem a bit lonely. How fascinating it would be if these inanimate objects, the ancient gold, the diamonds and precious stones could talk! How fiercely was the crown fought over, how many people died to gain it, how many were tortured in supporting it, how many kings died violently to keep it secure upon their heads! If a crown was capable of suffering, surely this one did, and bitterly. This is fact, not fancy.

Across the Palace Yard is the United Services Museum, and on the third side, the Scottish National War Memorial, reverence in stone and glass where those who died in two world wars, officers and other ranks, civilians in their homes, doctors, nurses, fire wardens and, even, mules and the humble miner's mouse are honoured for the great gift that they made to a grateful nation. The building is a living prayer and many a tear has been shed, and many a throat closes with grief, when the visitors reach the sanctuary where, laid on the rough out-cropping of the Castle Rock itself, is the great catafalque and casket containing the scrolls of names of those who died for their country in twentieth century battles.

Your guide has left you in front of the War Memorial and from there you are on your own. If the hour is early, you may enjoy a leisurely walk back down the twisting steps and paths of the Castle. You may choose to sit on a bench and absorb the atmosphere of this historic site, or lean on a parapet by Mons Meg and study the city from the sky. Take your time, whatever you do. The Castle will be there for a long time to come.

If, however, it is getting on toward lunch time, I suggest you saunter on down the Royal Mile as far as George IV Bridge, turn right down steep, curving Victoria Street and into Grass-

market. I could have sent you down Castle Wynd, but every time I
see that flight of ancient steps I think of Jack and Jill. So, let's take
it easily and go around. On the way, you might like to make a
slight detour via Candlemaker Row to Greyfriars Church. There,
outside the churchyard gate is the statue of Greyfriars Bobby, the
small terrier who stood guard beside the grave of his beloved
master until his own death fourteen years later. It's rather touch-
ing to dog lovers and when I am in Edinburgh I try to pass by the
faithful little fellow and consider for a moment the virtue, loyalty
and devotion that ask nothing in return.

Meals, in a rather stately and sacred procession, are of prime
importance to the Scots and since this is not a guidebook but my
own account of experiences and enjoyments, I shall from time to
time mention a restaurant – good ones that I think will enhance
your visit. There are many others, also good, from which to
choose but I am only going to cite ones of which I am particularly
fond. Thus, I have led you down to the Grassmarket. There you
will find The Beehive. The building itself is worth seeing and
quite in keeping with the spirit of your tour of the Old Town. If
you feel a need for a drink, there is a bar on the ground floor, but
before ordering your drinks you had best book a table since The
Beehive is very popular with businessmen as well as tourists. You
may find the menu a bit expensive, even though the food and
service is excellent, so if you are on a budget and see no reason to
splurge at luncheon, try the businessman's special, and have with
it a tankard of cider. Yes, cider, with a bit of apple floating in it,
can be had all over Scotland and is a grand accompaniment to a
lunchtime favourite of ours – the cold meat plate with salad.

After luncheon, return up Victoria Street and there you are
back on the Royal Mile. For the rest of the distance down the hill,
you're on your own with, I hope, guidebook in hand. I'll meet you
at the gates of Holyrood Palace, for the Royal Mile is a street
where you'll have a delightful time poking at will into whatever
interests you: cathedral, churches, houses, gift shops, antique
dealers, museums. It's all lined up for you.

But before we part, let me clear up two or three points that used
to confuse me.

I have constantly used the words The Royal Mile when referring to the street that runs down the ridge of the Old Town from

Castle Hill to Holyrood Palace. I have done that so you won't be confused. Now, to clear things up more precisely. Without your knowing it, this street has a habit of changing names as you go along. From the Castle Esplanade to the Tolbooth Church (properly Tolbooth St John's), the street is called Castle Hill. Then, it becomes the Lawnmarket. This is where the stalls were set up on market days. The High Street begins where the Lawnmarket leaves off at Bank Street and George IV Bridge. The Canongate begins at Leith Wynd, now called Cranston Street, and runs on down to Holyrood Palace. Not that this changes your route one whit, but it may explain why Lady Stair's House is in the Lawnmarket, St Giles and John Knox's House are on the High Street, and the Tolbooth is in the Canongate. Hence, the Royal Mile.

I have just mentioned Leith Wynd. You will see signs referring to 'Wynd', 'Vennel', and 'Close'. A 'close' is a blind alley, 'closed' off at one end. 'Wynd' and 'Vennel' are both the same thing: open alleys. A 'land' is a tall skinny house, a medieval skyscraper of often over ten stories. So much for some of the topographical peculiarities of the Old Town.

Holyrood Palace, at the bottom of the Royal Mile, is a splendid edifice in an equally splendid setting. After the narrow streets and alleys of the Old Town you are struck with the great openness of Holyrood Park. There, behind the lacy iron gateway, the pillars surmounted by the twin lions bearing the cross of St Andrew in their paws, is set the four-square palace. Behind are the gardens, and beyond, the slightly theatrical backdrop of Arthur's Seat (an extinct volcano) and the sheer cliff of Salisbury Crags.

'The Palace of Holyrood House' was begun, more or less, as a guest house when Holyrood Abbey was founded in 1128. It was added to, burned twice, rebuilt, torn down and again rebuilt. The present palace is a fine example of the Auld Alliance (French and Scottish) in architectural form. This is what we see today, the oldest part built by James IV (Mary, Queen of Scots' grandfather) and the newest the contribution of Charles II. Flanking the palace are the ruins, open to the sky, of the Chapel Royal, the relic of the old Holyrood Abbey built by King David, so the legend goes, as a penance for having gone stag hunting on a holy day. Of course, he got rather severely gored by a stag and one would think that penance enough; but in the middle of the night a voice told him to build a monastery on the spot where he was gored by the stag, and as any right-thinking man would react under those circumstances he did as he was told.

Since Holyrood Palace is an official residence of Her Majesty, visitors cannot roam about at will, but must go on a guided tour which is really very pleasant because the guides are most attractive young lassies. In addition to the present royal apartments and the historic rooms where Mary lived and Rizzio was murdered, one is taken through the Picture Gallery where Bonnie Prince Charlie held a triumphal ball under the eyes, 222 of them to be exact, of the 111 portraits of the rulers of Scotland from Fergus to James VI. These are the James de Witt portraits, ground out by the order of Charles II. If they are amusing, and they are, one must remember that poor de Witt was only allowed two years to complete this overwhelming order and he must be excused if he became hysterical once in a while. He hadn't the foggiest idea what these kings looked like, he was paid one hundred and twenty pounds sterling a year (which figures out at about two pounds a portrait) and he had to buy his own paints and canvas. It's too bad 'puir' de Witt was a Dutchman; a Scot would have driven a better bargain.

You've had enough walking for the day, so it's into a taxi with you and back to your hotel for tea or a drink, or both, and a good hot tub.

The second day should be spent in the New Town. There's a great variety of things to see and do. For shopping, there are the excellent stores along Princes Street and on both sides of George Street, in addition to the streets that connect the two: Castle, Frederick, Hanover, St David and St Andrew. There are fine speciality shops as well as large famous stores along these streets where you can find many of the products for which Scotland is renowned: tweeds, sweaters (called pullovers, jerseys or twinsets) in both lambswool and cashmere; crystal, pins and brooches set with cairngorms. In the larger stores foreign visitors should ask to be directed to the Export Department where trained personnel smooth the way for them.

All of these streets abound in restaurants and hotels where you may rest a bit and have a good lunch before starting out again. I could name some here, but since there are so many I don't think this would be quite fair. The City of Edinburgh Tourist Information Service puts out a leaflet (No. 3) that lists over sixty of them with complete descriptions and since they have done it so well there's no need for me to repeat it.

For a glimpse of how well-to-do Edinburgh lived (and *still* does to some extent) in the nineteenth century, roam at will through the streets that run behind George Street. You don't need a planned route; just wander as the spirit moves you and look upon the cool, classical face of the New Town.

There's not much to do in Edinburgh in the evening unless you are there during the Festival. Therefore, I suggest the following course of action because I can't stand the thought of visitors clinging to the American habit of a too-early dinner and then twiddling their thumbs in that most impersonal of all jails, the hotel bedroom. First, be sure to have a really good tea at about four or four-thirty. Then, if you're feeling energetic, hike up Calton Hill at the eastern end of Princes Street. The top of the hill is crowned with various pieces of architectural crockery which I try to ignore. In fact, I have the odd feeling that the city fathers put them there simply because there was no other place to put them, at least for the moment. As a result, they seem rather *pro tem*. There's only one reason for climbing up Calton Hill and that is the spectacular view you get for your pains. It really is lovely, especially in the late afternoon sunlight.

If you have a car, or are willing to hire a taxi, take an after-tea drive through Holyrood Park, following the circular Queen's Drive that winds up and around the base of Arthur's Seat and Salisbury Crags. As you climb higher, there are outlooks from which you can see in various directions, out over the city, over the Firth of Forth to the distant mountains, east to the sea and southwest toward the Pentland Hills. That is, of course, providing the weather is good and you can see at all!

After dinner, at a latish hour, you might want to indulge in one of our favourite after-dinner entertainments: people-watching on Princes Street. Be sure to put on a warm wrap and saunter – your feet are probably tired anyhow – down Princes Street, on the garden side. Sit occasionally, if you like, and watch the world go by. I won't attempt to describe it, for it changes from night to night. If, after a while you would like a night-cap, cross Princes Street and, one block behind and parallel, you'll find Rose Street. It looks like an alley – and is. Here are long lines of pubs, twenty-six at the latest count. Pick any one that appeals. But keep your eye on the clock. The bars get turned-off very early.

I realize now I have gone on a good deal about Edinburgh and, in spite of my good intentions, in travel book style. But I wanted to show you 'my' Edinburgh and I have only skimmed the surface. There is so much to see and to do. Perhaps I have only put your feet on the right path. I hope you will continue on, for 'my' Edinburgh will never disappoint you.

As the American novelist Kate Douglas Wiggin said in her farewell:

> I canna thole [bear] my ain town
>   Sin' I have dwelt i' this.

I quite understand how she felt.

7. Come Foul Or Fair

NEVER try to understand a Scottish weather report.

You may, as we do, turn on the radio first thing in the morning and as the last strains of the theme, Handel's 'Water Music', die away, you will be given a nicely enunciated but totally unintelligible weather report. You'll then snap off the radio and wonder just *what* that man said. The report will consist of a jumble of 'showeries, thunderings and sunny intervals'. You have no idea what the day is going to be like. Well, I have a bit of intelligence to pass along. That's just exactly what it's going to do: be showery and thundery with sunny intervals. In fact, I've never heard a Scottish weather reporter state that the day was going to be sunny, unequivocally sunny, all day long. But it does happen! The announcer, or the weatherman, or the B.B.C., just won't go out on such a slender limb to forecast it.

Next, you'll buy a newspaper and turn to the weather column. This is the most frustrating thing you could do. The report was written the night before and that's far too slow for Scottish weather. Then, you're faced with another problem. You have to know where you are. Of course, you know *that,* but you must know where you fall in the Scottish weather map.

This map is divided roughly into three, four or five sections, running on angles from south-west to north-east. I say 'roughly' because the sections tend to vary to suit the weather, but in the main they are (*a*) The Borders, (*b*) Edinburgh and E. Scotland, Aberdeen area, Central Highlands, Moray Firth area, (*c*) S.W. Scotland, Glasgow area, Argyll, (*d*) N.W. Scotland, (*e*) Orkney and Shetland. I must warn you that the categories change every day but this is a fairly usual arrangement. Now, you decide where you are and find that, for instance, the Glasgow area is slated for rain and East Scotland is promised 'bright periods' and there you are, right on the borderline, say in Stirling. What's going to happen? Anything! You'll never know until the day is over. Let us suppose you *were* in Stirling and you planned a day in the area, over to Callander and perhaps up to Loch Katrine. What kind of a day can you expect? Well, you'll probably have rain at breakfast-time, clearing as you climb in the car, bright sunshine on the streets of Callander, and a steady, thick, murky downpour as you reach the rain-obliterated shores of Loch Katrine. Or it might be all the other way around. It might rain while you're in a shop in Callander and be crystal clear, all white and blue and silver, at Loch Katrine.

I have purposely let a note of frenzy creep into all this because at first Scottish weather reports can put you into just that state. Weather *reports,* not necessarily Scottish weather!

Scottish weather is great, especially if you like surprises. We rather enjoy an experience such as a wet, gale force wind rocking the car parked beside the Royal and Ancient at St Andrews, cloudless skies driving through Cupar, a thunderstorm ten miles on at Auchtermuchty, a double rainbow at Milnathort, hail at the Yetts of Muckart, and a flaming sky reflected on Glen Devon as we dried out at the Dormie House at Gleneagles. That was all in the course of an hour's drive, mind you.

There is a scientific reason behind all of this meteorological backing and filling. And this is why the maps look as they do, why the reports make as much sense to you as the Dead Sea Scrolls, and why you come close to hysteria as you ponder what to wear and where to go for the day. My advice is to take a raincoat, dress

c

warmly, and don't let the weather influence your plans. There's a funny thing about Scottish weather: ignore it and it has a habit of going away. Pretend you like it and it will reward you with a sunny smile, at least for one of those 'bright periods'.

Scotland is at the northern end of an island in the Atlantic Ocean. This is of great importance. Nearly the size of the state of Maine, it is on the same latitude as Hudson's Bay. It is two hundred and seventy-five miles long and approximately one hundred and fifty miles wide. Out of a total of nineteen million acres, twelve million are from one thousand to over four thousand feet above sea level. The air can be pretty cold up there.

The prevailing winds are from the south-west and they are warmed by the Gulf Stream, which passes close to Scotland's western shores. When these warm, moist winds from the Caribbean area strike the mountains on the west coast of the country they are forced upwards and the cold upper air changes the moisture to rain. So much for Science! The point to all of this is that the heaviest rainfall is on the mountains north of the Firth of Clyde. Up there they can be the recipients of about eighty inches a year, with Glen Garry holding a dubious record of two hundred sopping, sloshing inches. In comparison, the east coast, with only thirty inches, is a positive Sahara. So that's why it rains a lot and why the weather map is cut on the diagonal, since that is the way the mountains run.

Scottish weather prophets don't make a big thing out of temperature, and with good reason. Since the highest (*highest,* mind you) *difference* between summer and winter is only 21.4 degrees and the *lowest* a paltry 16.2, there's really not a great deal to be said. The *average* temperature in winter is about thirty-four degrees and the *average* temperature in summer is about fifty-five degrees. Now you see why mothballs aren't a fast-moving item in Scotland, why old ladies never peel off their woollies and why seventy degrees is a heatwave.

In January and February – not big tourist months, I assure you – gale force winds blow one day out of every ten. Then, even the natives try to escape to Majorca or Portugal or Nassau.

There is one great difference between winter and summer, though. Winter gives the impression of being just one long night; and summer, one long day. In summer, I've seen golfers finish up a game at nine o'clock and witnessed many a sunset over Arran at ten-thirty. At Turnberry Hotel, where most guests dine around eight-thirty, the curtains have to be drawn to keep out the blazing sun. This is true, absolutely true, and I can't figure out *how* Freddie and I, driving back from a dinner party in Perthshire, before midnight, in July when the sky is still light, became hopelessly lost in total, confusing blackness and blundered about like rogue elephants on the rampage. So black was it that when we made a wrong turning we simply could not see the road in order to back up. It could have been the 'Islay Coffee', but I doubt it. It's really a matter I'd like to discuss with the science experts.

Now you know about all you need to know about Scottish weather. Prepare to be on the cool side and expect to be rained on. That way you'll not be disappointed. As to the 'Old Probabilities' on the radio, listen with amusement. Remember, everything they predict is going to happen, especially the 'showery periods'. Perhaps that is why the Scottish Home Service of the B.B.C. in its infinite wisdom chose 'Water Music' with which to begin a typical Scottish day.

8. *Roundabout*

AT SOME point during your visit to Scotland you may hear a reference made to 'diving by Braille'. At a cocktail or dinner party, it could mean the driver has had a bit much to drink and that he has, thank Heaven, a guardian angel upon whom to rely. Or the remark might be made on a foggy night, an annoyingly repetitive natural event in the Scottish countryside. You will probably be mystified.

The real explanation is simple and the reason most realistic and clever. In many places, the canny Scots had set down the absolute middle of their primary roads, a double row of heavy metal studs, thus dividing the road into two lanes. There is a painted marker line, certainly, but in the dark of night, or in a fog, natural or personal, these lines have a nasty way of disappearing as does, often, the entire road itself. However, if the driver successfully manages to place his car in the correct lane, the LEFT, he can drive along quite confidently if he keeps his right wheel just to the left of the studs. If he feels the studs under his tire, he has crossed into the wrong lane and must ease over again. All of the driving by Braille has only one drawback: one must be absolutely lynx-eyed for another car bowling along in the fog with *his* right wheels *on* the line of cleats. If the fog is self-induced, may I suggest an alert companion to be on sentry-go. Besides, it will make that manifestly highly nervous person feel necessary to the successful completion of the homeward trek and keep him (or more generally *her*) from clawing strips off of the upholstery. Better still, if intoxicated, don't drive at all, for Britain has introduced a device called a 'Breathalyser', to measure the alcoholic content of the driver, and this experiment has been most successful in cutting down accidents caused by drunken drivers. All visitors ought to cooperate with the local authorities in a most commendable project to save lives from road accidents.

Far too many tourists go to Scotland in a state of abject terror about the roads. They have been told at home that the roads in England are lanes with blind corners, an ever-present hazard to life and limb, and if this is so, it must be even more frightful in that rugged land 'up north'. This is not altogether the true picture. In England, there are lanes, but there are also super-highways the equal of anything elsewhere, and since the cars are not as high-powered, except for an Austin-Healey or an Aston-Martin or so with a demon at the wheel, the traffic moves at a far more intelligent pace. Scotland is no different. Avoiding the Ministry of Transport designations like the plague, the Scottish roads are classed as principal trunk highways, other roads for long distance traffic, important connecting roads, and other roads.

The 'principal trunk highways', a swath of red or red and yellow on the maps, are new, wide, often dual and always undergoing 'roadworks'. There are roughly four of them. One from Berwick-upon-Tweed to Edinburgh, a second from Gretna to Glasgow, one connecting Edinburgh and Glasgow, and another from Glasgow north to Perth and through the Highlands to Inverness. I say 'roughly' because others are being brought steadily up to this high standard.

'Other roads for long distance traffic' are equally fine – *in places* – and it is these roads that are being widened and made into principal trunk highways. Even as they are they are excellent.

'Important connecting roads' are the last category of highways marked heavily in red on your map and there's nothing wrong with them either, except that there's no passing lane and they do tend to wind about.

The roads traced in pale grey or a red hairline are the 'other roads'. This sounds rather formidable and *some* of them, no more than paved sheep-paths up hill and down dale, are shocking. But others (and we've driven over miles of them) are as good as the next higher classification. We believe in getting off the beaten path and taking short cuts. We never hesitate to use these roads, and we've only had one unfortunate experience. That was because of too much traffic on a road that should have been empty of all cars except for the local farmers' and ours. You see, many of the roads in the far north, way up in the Highlands, are single track. Now, this in itself is not as bad as it may sound. They are smoothly paved, immaculately groomed by old men who daily pick up the collections of trash tossed out by tourists and have, every fifty or one hundred yards, on alternate sides, 'lay-bys'. These are turn-outs where a polite driver will wait for an on-coming car to pass. Here there is no hard and fast rule about this, but merely a reliance upon common courtesy. So, if you are closer to a lay-by than another occupant of the road, it is your duty to pull off the road. If the on-coming vehicle is a big tourist bus or a van, especially a trailer truck (which is called an articulated lorry) give way out of self-preservation. Above all, don't drive too close to the vehicle ahead of you, because you have no idea what notions of courtesy its driver may have.

One last note to the driving tourist: be careful! Not overly cautious to the point of being a timorous menace, but simply *careful* and don't speed. Remember you are driving a car to which you are not accustomed, you are on what to you is the wrong side of the road, your wheels have a tendency, in town, to bounce off curbs as you turn corners and traffic circles – and these 'round-abouts', are sheer horror, for all of your instincts tell you to bear right when you MUST keep LEFT. With care and a bit of concentration at first you'll soon get the hang of it and it won't be long until you are driving like a veteran. In fact, one or two days should do it, especially if you can keep away from the heavily travelled roads. On our first trip it only took Freddie four tours around the car park at Prestwick Airport, a stop at every lay-by (supposedly to breathe the fresh air) between Ayr and Turnberry, and two large whiskies to celebrate our safe arrival, to become the picture of nonchalance. I admit he was a quivering jelly until after he had a shot of that liquid courage; but now, year after year, he drives by Braille with perfect insouciance and they no longer attach the 'Visitor To Britain' sticker in his back window. He rather feels that he has 'arrived'. That is, until my old vehicle has been passed by a snarling, flashing sports car on one of those 'Other Roads'.

9. The Cup That Cheers

WHISKY means only one thing in Scotland. It does not mean Bourbon or Irish or Rye. It means Scotch whisky. You can get the others, but you need to be specific when ordering them.

To drink whisky as the Scots do, ask for 'whisky and water' or 'whisky and splash', meaning a splash of soda. They'll probably ask tourists if they require ice, but if you really want to cut a figure, look aghast and say, 'No, thank you!' Ice has a tendency to freeze the taste buds and you'll miss a good deal of marvellous flavour.

You can order about anything your thirst desires: those other whiskies, gin with tonic, 'It' or a Pimm's Cup Number Whatever. Sherry is excellent, but I have discovered that it is far more potent per quantity than gin and whisky and I am not at all deluded by the attempts of nice old ladies, to give an impression of being nearly teetotallers, who say they'll take 'Just a small sherry'. They don't fool me for one minute, especially if they allow themselves to be coaxed into having just one more, 'but small, y'know'. I've had some rather stupefying experiences with a nip or two of sherry and in the interests of sobriety I'll take whisky every time.

The word whisky is Celtic in origin. It comes from the words 'uisge beatha', contracted to 'usquebaugh' meaning 'water of life'. There are at least eight modern Scots ways of spelling this old Gaelic word but 'whisky' will do perfectly for ordering purposes.

In Scotland whisky means, naturally, a great deal more than just something to drink in a Scottish bar or at home. What is far more important is that it is drunk in bars and homes all over the *world,* for whisky is the prime commodity in Scotland's export trade. In fact, I sometimes get the feeling that the Scots consider whisky to be rather sacred, which it is indeed for a variety of reasons, all of which are quite obvious.

Scotch whisky is of two kinds. One is made in a pot still, the other in a patent still. Roughly, the process is as follows. The 'wort', fermented grain and malt, produces a weak solution of alcohol. This solution, now called the 'wash' is placed in a large copper still, a vat which can hold about four thousand gallons at a time. A long, narrow, coiled tube forms the neck of the still and passes through a tank of cold water. When the liquid in the still is heated the alcohol in the mixture boils at a much lower temperature, of course, than does the water. When the alcohol vapour passes through the cold tubing it condenses and becomes liquid once more. This process of distilling is repeated several more times until only pure alcohol is left. Elementary, of course. Before it becomes potable whisky, the liquid is left to mature in old sherry, or other well-seasoned, casks for a period of from three to fifteen years.

In a pot still, the wort consists of barley mixed with malt. In patent stills the wort may be compounded of corn (maize), barley, rye and oats. Maize, which is not used in pot stills, is the principal ingredient.

The pot stills in Scotland produce four types of whiskies: the Highland malts which come mostly from Speyside or the Glenlivet region; the Lowland malts; Islay, which has a strongish taste because the malt has been cured over peat fires; and, last, Campbeltown, of which flavour is even more pronounced than that of Islay.

Whisky from a patent still does not have as wide a range of flavour as do the whiskies from pot stills. This may be because the malt cured over peat fires is not used.

The blending of whisky in Scotland is becoming a fairly universal practice and the reasons for this are simple: a standard flavour can be achieved and a cheaper product can be produced. These blends are considered best if the formula consists of half Highland and Lowland malt, a small amount of Islay and the rest patent still whisky. Even as I write this I can hear contentious voices being raised. I wonder if any two Scotch whisky drinkers would ever agree about the right blend?

Freddie and I once visited a famous distillery in the Lowlands and we were flabbergasted to discover that the blending of the various grains was done completely by automation: flashing lights on a large board, watched over by one man. I must say some of the romance was taken out of the procedure, but I'm all for progress. The rest of the distillery was of standard operation and the odour of raw alcohol, grain and malt was rather overpowering, as were the huge vats, the cat-walk connections and spider-work ladders, over and up which my timid feet had to pick their cautious way. I was an utter wreck when we arrived at the manager's office and were rewarded with a finger or two of the finished product, which bore no resemblance to the witches' brew roiling and stewing in the obscure reaches of the distillery.

It all sounds very unromantic to those who prefer the idea of stills hidden away in mountain glens and watched over by hundreds of ghostly pipers, but I like to know what I am drinking and a visit to a distillery certainly convinces the non-initiated that the Scots know what they're doing.

'Doch-an-Dorris', or 'Deuch-an-Dorach', is a phrase you may hear when with friends. It means to have one-for-the-road. Don't! Especially if you're driving.

10. The 'Other' Place

WHAT can I say about Glasgow? In all honesty, that is – so that visitors aren't led up the garden path and I am not *tobered* (as in *tobermor* axe) by the next Glaswegian I meet. Glasgow has to take enough smacks in the eye without my adding to it. After all, Glasgow is a part of Scotland and its peculiarities add their textures and colours to the tapestry that is Scotland. Glasgow is the oldest and largest city in Scotland and the centre of its economic life. That is hardly damning it with faint praise. But, let's look at it from a visitor's standpoint. (And by St Mungo, it's hard to be objective!)

Glasgow is a city where you notice people. Edinburgh is a city where history and ancient monuments make people fade into mere shadows. In Edinburgh people are terribly snobbish, especially about Glasgow. In Glasgow, the people go about with their fists cocked, ready to take physical revenge for slights on their city. They're always on the defensive, and I imagine they have plenty of good reasons. Even after many years away from the banks of the Clyde, a Glaswegian sticks out in an expatriate crowd like a sore thumb. They're always the ones who sing along, misty-eyed, to every Harry Lauder tune or clap and shout enthusiastically to Will Fyffe's song, 'I Belong To Glasgow'.

I belong to Glasgow, dear old Glasgow town!
   But what's the matter with Glasgow?
For it's going round and round.
   I'm only a common old workin' chap, as any one can see,
But when I get a couple of drinks on a Saturday,
   Glasgow belongs to me.*

Overseas, you'll seldom find an expatriate Glaswegian decked out in kilt and Argyll jacket. The population takes its tone from the highly independent transplanted Highlanders who came to the city to seek the high wages of industry and the even more independent translated Irishmen who came to the city for the same purpose. On the whole both of these groups were highly successful and their attitudes, at home and abroad, are the epitome of 'Wha's like us!'

If you'd care to see this particular facet of Glasgow's personality in violent action, attend a football (soccer) game some Saturday afternoon. But you must be hardy, fleet of foot and not overly weak-stomached about the fisticuffs that break out among the spectators, especially when Celtic are playing Rangers. Glaswegians are 'fitba' mad'. Purchase good seats, preferably near an exit, try not to take a female companion, and above all, watch the game in stony silence. Don't even make a passing remark of seemingly innocuous nature to another spectator or you might become a candidate for the St John's Ambulance Brigade. I should hate to think of your tour ending at Ibrox Park or Parkhead, so keep your opinions to yourself.

Beyond the city's boast of great industry, philanthropic merchants, hard-working people and championship football teams, it is also the site of the great Glasgow University, founded in 1450,

*Copyright 1921 Francis, Day & Hunter, Ltd., London. Renewed 1948, Leeds Music Corp., N.Y.

where some of the world's finest doctors and engineers have been trained. Both of my physicians are products of the university's faculty of medicine and, though I regret the brain-drain, I am grateful to Glasgow for this fine institution.

The tourist who enjoys good food and the conviviality of the pub will enjoy the city, for the restaurants are of the best and there are over one thousand pubs – *not one* of them a suitable place in which to discuss the merits of any football team. There are several excellent theatres and concert halls, reputedly the best British art gallery outside of London, and fine shops, mostly located in a street laughingly referred to as the 'Rue de Sauchiehall'. (Always pronounced 'sawk-ee-haw').

Beyond the thirteenth century cathedral and the Tron Steeple, there's not a surfeit of sightseeing to be done. An invidious comparison must be made with Edinburgh in this respect, unless you have an eccentric penchant for Victorian architecture.

I really do think I have achieved objectivity, which is more than a lot of guide books can maintain with their references to bus tours for a 'quick look at the city' (translation: that's all that's necessary) and to the number of 'escape routes' (*their* phrase, not mine) out of the city to the beauties of the Ayrshire coast, locally called the 'Costa Clyde', and north toward Loch Lomond. So, if the guide books can afford such lapses, so may I be subjective just once and say that we prefer to pass through Glasgow as rapidly as possible, without getting lost, on a Sunday morning when there is little traffic, and route signs and street names can be read with sufficient ease to whisk you out of town as expeditiously as possible. One really can't go *around* Glasgow when going north or south on the lovely west coast of Scotland and since it is very easy to become muddled in the heart of the city this 'going straight through' takes a good bit of concentration. In fact, when such an ordeal is necessary, I develop a case of nerves for several days in advance, especially when approaching from the south. I pore over the city map like a general plotting battle and by the time we pass through Kilmarnock, a full twenty-one miles away, I have reached a cataleptic state and am only capable of muttering through clenched teeth, 'If Glasgow Bridge is the one the map shows us crossing why do we always find ourselves on King George V Bridge?' But somehow, 'by holding my mouth right', as

Freddie calls it, we always seem to find our way to the Great Western Road or Royston Road without too much retracing of steps. And yet, I wonder, *why* are we so leary of actually getting lost? Why *not* spend a few hours in great Glasgow? It might be very interesting.

Soon now the new bridge at old Erskine Ferry will make it possible to flit around Glasgow by crossing the Clyde farther downstream. I don't think we shall use it. I'd really *hate* to by-pass 'dear old Glasgow Town'.

11. A Short Geographic Glossary

(Note: G = Gaelic spelling)
Carse – flat, sometimes marshy, land near a river
Firth – an estuary
Ben – Beinn (G) – a mountain peak
Inch – an island in a river
Eilean (G) – an island
Burn – a brook
Kyle – a strait, or narrows
Balloch – a mountain pass
Corrie – a hollow in a mountain side, sometimes a mountain pool
Dun – a fort
Drum – a ridge
Glen – a valley
Inver – the mouth of a river, or the confluence of two rivers, or a
    river and a loch
Knock – a small hill, a knoll
Law – a hill
Loch – a lake
Tober – a well
Brig – a bridge
Scaur – a cliff
Torr – a hill
Mull – a promontory or headland
Muir – a moor
Strath – a plain
Lochan – a small lake or pool

Brae – a hillside
Beg – Beag (G) – small
Sma' – small
Yett – a gate
Mor – Mar (G) – big, large
Kil – a church
Watter (or water) – a river
Linn – a waterfall, or part thereof, precipice, cascade or pool at
  the base
Dubh (or Dhu) (G) – black
Auch – a field
Auchter – upland
Bal – township
Tay – Tigh (G) – house
Bane – Ban (G) – white
Gorm (G) – blue

As much caution should be exercised in pronouncing Scottish
place names as is used in picking up a horned toad. Be careful
how you grab it, if indeed you want to touch it at all.

A knowledge of the glossary above, which is as short as is
seemly, will aid greatly in your attempts to pronounce some of the
places you visit. Since the accent is invariably placed on the wrong
syllable, I make it a habit to inquire before I blast forth with any
new and novel pronounciation of centuries-old names. If you do
come a cropper, the kindly Scots will always offer a polite correc-
tion in a soft voice. As an example, because of a brand of sweater,
most Americans pronounce Braemar as *Brae*-mar. Because of its
meaning, it is obviously pronounced Brae-*mar*.

This is the only rule for pronounciation that I can give you, for
it is the only one I can lay hands on. But when in doubt, ask.

12. *The Poet And The Pig*

AYRSHIRE is the land of Burns and bacon and I am quite certain
that of the two I prefer the bacon, which is in itself a symbol of this
peaceful countryside, of its prosperous farms, rich potato fields,
rolling green hills speckled with sheep and glimpses of a sparkl-
ing sea. I find all of this far more poetic than the poet.

There's this to be said about writing a book. You may express your own opinions and you needn't expect to be agreed with on every point. In fact, I can already imagine the howls of indignation that will arise when I state quite bluntly that I think Robert Burns is highly over-rated. Millions of visitors come each year from all over the world to worship at the various shrines of Burns, and I often wonder why. I'm not about to launch into a diatribe on whether or not he was a saint or a sinner. I've suffered through too many tedious speeches, extolling his virtues or excusing his vices, all alleged, all second or third-hand source, at Burns' Nicht Suppers, to become involved in that completely irrelevant anachronistic matter. Burns was a man of his time, a man of the earth and the earthy, a man of poverty who had the misfortune to have been born a genius in an atmosphere, a social clime, where it was preferred that a genius be socially acceptable. Polite society, the ones who bought volumes of poetry, didn't readily take up farmer poets with dirt under their fingernails and the aroma of the barnyard about their persons. Not that Burns was not for a tragically short time a literary lion in Edinburgh, but the very fact that it did not last proves my point. Burns himself never became reconciled to the drawing-room. It might also be added here that Burns was the voice of the common *Lowland* Scot; but even then he wasn't speaking for all of the common men. They never had such thoughts as he had. Neither was he their hero. For the thirty-five years that he lived, he was simply one of them. He worked the fields as they did and drank on Saturday nights as they did, but he had this *gey* peculiar streak for writing poetry. I doubt if the hard-working farmers felt there was any poetry about their lives. It was all rather drab and monotonous. They were born, they laboured, they begat children, they died, and then their children picked up the identical lives that they had left off. They had no time nor inclination to write verses about field mice, daisies and blackbirds, let alone bannocks made of barley!

This prolific poet was not a man out of his time and place, either. He wrote about the things, some of them simple, some of them mystical and complex, that he either saw about him or thought about. I don't think he expected to bring about social change in a time when reforms were badly needed and I don't think he wrote his songs and ballads with any idea of gaining immortality. There are many who will argue these points, I know. As far as I can see, and I certainly was not there – nor were any of the scholars who are so clinically erudite about Burns – that the poet sang because it was essential to him, as natural as any other body function. Burns was a complete natural. He himself said that the poet is born, not made.

Now, the Lowland Scots who for many generations have been able to read and have had the leisure to do so are about the only people in the world who, in all honesty, can really *read* Burns. When I say 'read', I mean actually pick up a volume of his works and read any poem straight through with no strange words to mystify them. The only other group of such readers would be the *bona fide* Burns scholars. As to the rest of the world – the school-boys who receive his collected poems as a book prize, the Scots three generations removed from the land of their forebears, even university students, and some teachers – I am not at all persuaded that they can pick a poem at random and have the foggiest notion what it all means without recourse to a Scots dictionary. And to me, that is not reading poetry. The flow and the essence is lost.

Granted, Burns could write in pure English, but this is not the style and form we associate with Burns; and indeed, the majority of his work was written in broad Scots, or Lallans, as you prefer.

Take such words as *thrang, messin, tawted, duddie, stroan't, sheugh, sonsie, bawsn't, towzie, gawcie, hurdies, snowkit, moudie-worts, howkit, daffin', knowe, gash.* These words are all from the opening verses of one poem, and only the introduction at that. Does the average person have any idea what they mean? And how does one enjoy a poem when every other word draws a complete blank? I have a fairly decent knowledge of Scots and I find Burns tough going. After each abortive attempt I decide that any further reading must wait until my vocabulary is far more extensive. Poetry should be an emotional experience, not a scholarly exercise. Even Burns himself would have preferred it that way.

Therefore, my point is that the enraptured visitors to Burns' birthplace and the non-Scottish guests who listen with studied expressions to Burns' Nicht Supper readings, have read very little Burns, and at least only the poems that made him famous: 'Tam O'Shanter', 'The Jolly Beggars', 'The Cotter's Saturday Night', 'The Holy Fair', and 'The Twa Dogs'.

So much for Robert Burns the Poet. Now, let us look at what is called the Burns Country, certainly as lovely an inspiration for a rustic poet as exists anywhere in the world. This 'country' stretches from the town of Ayr south to the town of Dumfries. Between the two towns lie villages, hills and valleys, taverns and farms, all made famous by Burns' poems.

The first part of Burns' life, as the pendulum of creativity rose, was lived in the vicinity of Ayr. The town itself has very definite association with Burns' works for there is the old bridge of his 'The Brigs of Ayr' and there, also, is the Tam O'Shanter Inn. Ayr is a most pleasant town and certainly worth a visit by the Burns enthusiast. The Station Hotel is as good a spot as any for a meal and just in front of the hotel is the poet's statue for the worshipful to gaze upon.

Mecca, for the tourist, is naturally the cottage in Alloway, about two miles south of Ayr, where the poet was born on a January day in 1759. Here again I go slightly hay-wire on the subject of Burn-siana because this chilly, dreary cottage should be out in a field or at least on a narrow dirt road, *not* flanked by an enormous car park with a macadam highway a scant four feet from its minute windows. The tea rooms and gift shops that face it are almost an affront to one's sensibilities. I know they would be a shock to Burns himself. Frankly, I am left with the feeling that the cottage was really picked up from a far more pastoral setting and put down in the middle of this commercialism. It just looks all wrong.

However, here the lovers of Burns and those who feel it is their cultural duty to display an interest may enter the turnstile for the price of five pence and browse to their heart's content or as long as the tour guide lets them do so. For our part, we couldn't leave soon enough for we found the place vastly depressing and as Freddie said, 'If Burns took to drink, I wouldn't blame him.' This remark is, of course, beyond the realm of possibility for he left the clay cottage at the age of seven and, even solid man with the bottle that he was, he didn't begin *that* early.

A bit further down the road are more Burns landmarks. First is the church of Alloway and the Brig o'Doon, both prominent fea-tures of 'Tam O'Shanter' and his adventures. The last is the Burns Monument: for some occult reason, a Grecian temple set in a garden. It is here at this memorial that one may see Jean

Armour's wedding ring, a bit of metal, a reminder of the ties that bind which comes as much of a surprise to the modern visitor, considering Burns' flitting and sipping among the opposite sex, as it must have come to poor long-suffering Jean.

The second half of Burns' life, half in the sense of the downward swing of his health, following his sojourn in Edinburgh, and his marriage to Jean Armour, was passed in the south, in Dumfries-shire. Here he lived on a farm called Ellisland on the banks of the River Nith and later in the town of Dumfries itself, where he became an excise officer, wrote some of his most famous poems, met his friends at the Globe Inn, died and was buried in a mausoleum in St Michael's churchyard.

But it is not Dumfries-shire that one most commonly associates with Burns. It is Ayrshire, a rather large county that offers much to the visitor. I am very fond of Ayrshire and some of my happiest days are spent in its seaside towns and villages, driving up into the kindly hills behind Girvan and down along the River Stinchar and its deep salmon pools. The coast from the village of Ballantrae all the way to Troon and Ardrossan is most attractive and quite different from one's mental pictures of Scotland. Between Ballantrae at the mouth of the Stinchar and Girvan the road follows the very rocky edge of the sea and one can see – if one can see at all – south to the Giant's Causeway on the north coast of Ireland, Ailsa Craig, called Paddy's Milestone, and north to the island of Arran. All along here are the ruined castles of the once-powerful Clan Kennedy. Above Girvan is Turnberry with its famous hotel and even more famous championship golf courses. This is where Freddie rises at dawn and disappears to do battle with one or the other of these two formidable links. Links, by the way, is used in Scotland to differentiate between two types of golf courses. The seaside courses, rough, wind-swept and sandy, are called links. Nearby is Culzean Castle (pronounced Cul-*lane* or, better still, Cul-*yane*) which is open to the public and was the Scottish home of the late President Eisenhower. What that means is that the eighteenth-century castle, now a National Trust Property, has been divided into flats, one of which was set aside for the use of the former Supreme Allied Commander during his lifetime as a gesture of gratitude by the Scottish people. A visit to the gardens is worthwhile, for here in this northern island

Edinburgh: Floodlighting, Edinburgh Castle and Tattoo

Edinburgh: The Castle from the Scott Monument

Sgurr nan Gillean, Skye

Loch Lomond at Ardlui

you will see that palm trees do grow there – but you'd better take a picture to prove it!

North of Ayr are Prestwick and the golfer's destination, Troon. Between Troon and Largs are a series of seaside resorts – bathing beaches, pavilions, hotels and yacht basins – that have earned this seaside stretch the nicknames of the 'Costa Clyde' or the Scottish Riviera.

Inland, the northern countryside and towns have little to recommend them to tourists unless they have an absolute passion for coalfields, slag heaps and carpet mills. Here and there are a few famous whisky distilleries which might excite some interest and a trip through such plants can be easily arranged. But let me warn you, such is the odd aroma that it might turn you against whisky forever. Even this small area in the northern corner of the county, a tiny pocket that is nothing like the rest of beautiful, bountiful Ayrshire, has its Burns associations: Irvine where he worked for two years as a flax-dresser, and Kilmarnock where the first volume of his poems was printed.

In Ayrshire there's just no getting away from Burns, but on the whole, upon due consideration, I still prefer a breakfast plate full of delicious, lean, crisp Ayrshire bacon. It could make a poet out of me! Why, I could say it was *gey louable lardun* fit for a *syvewarm,* with *goggies sae byous geenyoch.* I could become *pootchin!*

Now, what was I saying about Burns?

It must be the Ayrshire air!

13. Dance For Joy

WHEN I happen to mention to people – and I do wish I wouldn't – that Freddie and I do Scottish Country Dancing, the all-too-inevitable rejoinder is, 'Oh, you can do the Highland Fling!' No, I cannot do the Highland Fling. I couldn't do it if my life depended on it. Neither could Freddie. We don't do the Sword Dance (the *Gillie Chalium*) either. Nor the *Seann Triubhas.* I can just barely pronounce that one! This is Highland Dancing, intricate, highly technical, generally associated with military display groups and boys and girls, competition medals bouncing on their chests, at Highland games.

D

What I'm talking about is Scottish Country Dancing. This is ballroom dancing done in assembly rooms, county residences, barns, town halls, hunt balls and gymnasiums all over Scotland. In fact, it is done the world over, wherever Scots get together. Even so, it is not considered folk dancing, in the truest sense of the word. It began at Court and was adopted, and adapted, by the common people. Many of the steps come from Highland dancing and the foot positions come from classical ballet, but these are not matters that worry the enthusiastic dancer. Scottish Country Dances are reels, jigs, hornpipes, strathspeys and medleys of reel and strathspey.

In your travels you will probably see Highland Dancing, especially at the Edinburgh Tattoo or at Highland games, but I do hope you have the opportunity of seeing Scottish Country Dancing, which is experiencing a re-birth through the efforts of its patron saint, Miss Jean C. Milligan, co-founder of the Royal Scottish Country Dance Society. At the major hotels, the resort type in the country, a Saturday night's dancing will include a piper or two playing for a bit of the traditional dancing. However, this will not be the art in its finest form, believe me.

For one reason, pipes are grand, but they are difficult to dance to and the proper music should be provided by an accordion, a violin, a bass, plus, perhaps, a cello, piano and drums. However, one can get along quite merrily with an accordion and fiddle.

Another reason is that the dances as executed in the hotels are rather limited. The first choice is likely to be 'The Gay Gordons', reputedly an English dance, which is a neither-here-nor-there sort of thing. The other will be 'The Eightsome Reel', which is complicated and strenuous and in the hotels is generally so badly done that it becomes a shambles.

The third reason, and the major contribution to the chaos of the second reason, is that the dances are chiefly done, if that is the word I want, by the Sassenachs, people up from England for the season who may have been exposed to it in their schools as part of physical education. It's all rather wretched.

To see such dancing well done you will have to go into the country where dance exhibition teams often perform at gatherings and fairs.

As you watch, you may think that it's like square dancing. Up to a point, it is, since the Scots who came to America in the eighteenth and nineteenth centuries brought it with them and with time it changed in many ways. 'The Virginia Reel' is a direct descendent.

The differences lie in the footwork and, also, in the fact that American square dancing has a caller who sings out, like a tobacco auctioneer, the movements as they come along. This sounds a bit like cheating in Scottish Country Dancing since the patterns and formations of each dance must all be memorized. There are well over two hundred well-known dances, with new ones coming along and gaining in popularity, and this takes a bit of doing. When invited to dance 'The Duke of Perth' or 'The Lea Rig' or 'The Montgomeries' Rant', you hear the opening chord for bow and curtsey, and then it's sink or swim. In small social groups you may get a quick read-through, but that is all. At a ball, nary a word is spoken. This is not a deterrent. It literally keeps you on your toes, mentally and physically.

Dance societies exist in the major cities of the United States and Canada, and visitors from the New World might enjoy joining such a group on their return home. It takes about six months of weekly dancing to learn the rudiments and another six months to un-muddle yourself, but all of the time it is great fun and wonderful exercise. That is to say, after your heart learns to take it in stride and your indigestion subsides. Inquiries as to groups at home can be made through The Royal Scottish Country Dance Society at 12 Coates Crescent in Edinburgh. Your local paper at home may carry a class listing or if there is a St Andrews or Caledonian Society in your city they may be able to inform you.

14. So To Speak

THERE ARE three languages in Scotland: English (King's or Queen's), Scots or Lallans, and Gaelic.

Scots, the language used by Robert Burns, is common in many dialectic variations throughout Scotland, but those who speak in this broad Scots also speak plain English, so you'll have no problem.

Gaelic is a horse of a totally different colour. Forget it. There's no need to rush out to a professional language school for a quick course. I'm certain that there are few, if any, outside Scotland. Furthermore, Gaelic is not a 'plume de ma tante' sort of language.

There are very few people in Scotland today with whom you might strike up a matey conversation in Gaelic, even if you did take the trouble to make a stab at the language. Back in 1951 someone, I'll never know who, conceived the idea of taking a census on the number of people who spoke Gaelic in Scotland. The findings must have depressed him a good deal, for out of a population of over five million people only 0.05 per cent spoke only Gaelic (I'd love to know where *they* are lurking) and 1.80 per cent spoke both Gaelic and English. Most of today's 80,000 people who speak Gaelic live in the counties of Argyll, Inverness, Ross and Cromarty and Sutherland. This includes the Inner and Outer Hebrides, for interestingly enough, of these islands eight belong to Ross and Cromarty, forty-four to Inverness-shire and forty to Argyllshire. The largest island is divided in two: Harris belonging to Inverness-shire and the larger part, Lewis, to Ross and Cromarty.

The Gaelic language, also called Erse, has a history of ups and downs. It was brought to Scotland by the original Scots, the Goidelic Celts from Ireland who settled on the western coast. Ireland was at that time called Scotia. Gradually, the language spread to cover the whole land north of the Clyde and the Forth.

Below this line, the waist-band of Scotland, a language that was largely English was spoken and when this southern part of what is now modern Scotland was conquered from the north, a Gaelic speaking government ruled over a mass of people who spoke English. I simply cannot refrain from adding here, for your edification, that a large part of the subjugation of the Angles was accomplished by the seventh century King of the Picts, named Brude MacBile. Then, Malcolm Canmore, Malcolm Big-Head, married an exiled English princess and, thus, in the eleventh century, English was introduced officially to the Scottish court. Malcolm's queen, Margaret, eventually St Margaret, was a highly religious woman and it was most inconvenient to discover that the Scottish prelates with whom she intended to do a great deal of business spoke Gaelic. So, for a time, 'English' or 'Inglis' was the language of polite society. However, in the fifteenth century there was an official Gaelic revival and when James IV founded King's College at Aberdeen, the use of English was prohibited. By the time his great-grandson, James VI came along, the brief days of glory for the Gaelic were over. The reasons were P.P.E.: Political, Practical and Expedient. James VI had become King of England also, and it seemed a good idea to suppress the Gaelic language and culture as a means of cutting down to size the Highland chiefs and their gangs of loyal adherents who were getting too big for their kilts which could no longer be called *philabegs.*

This effort was not a huge success because, one, the word did not get around the hills and glens with any rapidity and, two, the stubborn, kingly chiefs felt that what James *Saxt* didn't hear, wouldn't bother him. So, as late as 1800 Gaelic was spoken by high and low alike all over the northern Highlands. But, then, Scots canniness took over. The not-so-foolish Scots realized that in order to survive they were duty-bound to beat the English, if not in battle, then by the power of economics and political position. In order to do this, they had to speak the same language. So, they put their obstinate minds to learning English and, as a result, through language rather than force of arms, many Scots came down out of the hills to attain high places in government and fame, through political, scientific and financial achievements, the world over.

Today, a keen interest is being displayed in Gaelic and in Celtic culture among both the wealthy aristocracy, whose ancestors saw the light and learned English, and the young of all classes who are looking to the past for cultural enrichment. A Gaelic Mod is now held each year in Scotland for singing and poetry, chairs of Celtic culture and studies have been established at universities, people of all ages gather to hold a Ceilidh (kay-lee), an informal sing-along of old Gaelic tunes, songs and mouth-music. What practical end all this has I have no idea and neither do any Scots whose heads are not lost in clouds as high as those around Ben Nevis. Scotland must look forward and not backward.

Several years ago, in spite of Freddie's scoffing, I ordered several books that were supposed to permit the self-teaching of Gaelic with a minimum of mental agony. After weeks of heroic concentration, I gave up. To admit to failure in learning a language was to me, a fair linguist, a shocking blow to mind and spirit. Gaelic, as far as I am concerned, will never be self-taught.

What I need is an entire faculty of grey-bearded Celtic scholars. Perhaps, with their undivided attention, I might make head or tail of this fantastic, nightmarish language. Of course, what really irritates me is that an un-tutored shepherd on the hills (wherever *he is*) can speak it with facility; and Freddie, who insists that I should eventually tackle this linguistic puzzle, hastens to point out such noisome facts to me. Perhaps someday I will make another attempt, but this time I shall have that wretched shepherd at my side. Then I shall *'Abair ach beag is abair gu maith e'* or 'Say little, but say it well.'

Just to show you what one is up against I'll give you a few examples from these 'Gaelic-Made-Easy' traps. You're off to a rousing start, at least *I* was, when you discover early on in the books that the plural possessive of 'you' is 'at you.' So far, so good. Then, you're in immediate trouble. 'At you' breaks down to *aig*, pronounced 'ek', meaning 'at' and *sibh*, pronounced 'sheev', meaning 'you', plural. Then the two words *aig* and *sibh* combine to become *agaibh*, pronounced 'akeev'.

Another book begins right off the bat with a study of ellipses according to various districts before you've even learned *one* dialect. In one section they advised me that *an do ghabh thu e* became *ar Dia*, pronounced 'ur nea'. Now *really!*

Then, there's the designation of clan chiefs and chieftains to be considered. One was made to feel that they would prefer to be called by their Gaelic names. This is not really true, I feel, having known a few chiefs and chieftains in my time. How could I possibly refer to Campbell of Glenorchy as 'Mac-Chailein-'ic Dhonnachaidh' or McLaine of Lochbuie as 'Sliochd Mhurchaidh Ruaidh'. Sir Gregor MacGregor of MacGregor, Bt, The MacGregor, will remain just *that* as far as I am concerned and not 'An t' Ailpeanach'.

Even if I were to learn Gaelic, and I will, it must either be a spoken or a written language. I shall learn to speak it fluently without the foggiest notion of how to spell it, since the spelling and pronunciation of a Gaelic word seem to be totally unrelated, *or* I shall read poetry and folk tales, but I'll never open my mouth to say so much as 'Thank you' since no Gaelic speaking person would understand what I was saying should I attempt *Gu'n robh maith agad.*

It all goes to prove that as simplified and inexpensive as are the self-teaching Gaelic grammars, you can't learn a language for forty pence no matter how appealing it might be to anyone with a thrifty drop of Scots blood. If anyone could, it would be the greatest bargain known to modern man.

Scots or Lallans (Lowland Scots) is another thing altogether. In fact, I do quite well with Scots because all you need is to gain a vocabulary and remember a few small matters in regard to pronunciation.

'Ng' which is found in many English words used in Scots is pronounced like 'ng' in 'singer' – 'sing–er' – *not* 'sin–ger'. Thus, 'hunger' is 'hung–er', 'finger' is 'fing–er'. The other important point is that 'zie' in a word is pronounced like 'ni' in 'onion' or the 'll' in William. Hence, the name Menzies is correctly pronounced 'Ming–ies'. The rest of the pronunciations lean more toward that of Continental Europe rather than that of England. The English have the habit of dropping or slurring 'r'. The Scots give it a full measure of attention.

Scots is also spoken somewhere below where one's tonsils are supposed to be and this is called the 'glottal stop'. Even to say the word 'glottal' gives one a pretty good idea of what it should sound like. In this way, the word 'ridiculous' emerges as 'rri–duck-u-lus'. Then, too, the Scots have a funny habit of transposing letters: 'griddle' becomes 'girdle' and 'together' is 'thegither'. All of which makes learning to speak in good broad Scots a great deal of fun.

You may wonder, now, just where 'Scots' came into the linguistic picture. This is a choice example of nationalism. It's really not Scots at all. The Scots spoke Gaelic or Erse. 'Old Scots' was a regional dialect that was spoken around Edinburgh, in the Lothian counties, at court and in the universities at certain periods of history. It was based upon English (the people on the south-eastern coast of Scotland being Angles), Latin from the clergy and law courts, and French from the Auld Alliance. Scots is a language that grew rather like Topsy, and today's Scots consists of English words, invented words, Anglicized Gaelic words and words borrowed through trade, alliance and wars from Dutch, French, Norse, Polish and German. The veneer of adapted Gaelic words is especially heavy. So, there were these people with a language that had developed in the lowlands of Scotland and was properly called Lallans but which, for nationalistic reasons, they chose to call Scots simply because it was the language spoken by the majority of the people living in a kingdom called Scotland. Scotland, in turn, had taken its name or had its name imposed upon it by a group of people from Ireland who had settled on the west coast and who eventually brought the whole land under its political control, when Malcolm II conquered the Lothians.

There you have the three languages of Scotland and I could be quite happy with two if it weren't for the third. In fact, I've become rather unhinged by the Gaelic. Such is my fixation that I find myself listening for it whenever I am far away north in the Highlands. I've found that group of Gaelic speakers highly elusive and I've carried my search to rather inane extremes upon several occasions. I remember one night at dinner at the Kyle of Lochalsh, facing across to the island of Skye, when Freddie and I, with seven languages between us, listened to the hushed conversation of two bright-cheeked, black-haired waitresses. 'There,' said I to Freddie somewhat triumphantly. 'They're speaking Gaelic!' Rather than let me bask contentedly in a glow of victory at last, the dear man turned to the girls and asked if it was the Gaelic they were speaking. 'Oh, no, sir,' one replied. 'It's French.'

15. St Peter Of The Revolving Door

IN SCOTLAND, the hotel hall porter is an institution, a fact best recognized early on. He is the source of all knowledge and the judge of all guests. He knows to whom to bow, ever so slightly, and whom to fix with the fishy-eyed stare. While at once giving the impression that nothing happens in the hotel that he is not informed about, that he is the brimming fountain of information of local affairs, he has the uncanny knack of pretending that he has never seen before a year-in-year-out guest about whom he has reservations known only to himself; and, on the other hand, of greeting with a modicum of grace, which passes with him as wild enthusiasm, an acceptable guest who has not darkened the hotel's entry in several years. He is not affected by wealth, and a noble rank does not move him to more than icy civility and the correct use of a title, unless the possessor has 'the right attitude'. 'The right attitude' implies a respect for his office, not spending an undue amount of time in the 'American bar', an air of decorum in the lounge after dinner and no 'hanky-panky'. He desires his guests to be married if possible, to have a nodding acquaintance with certain other select guests, to arive with a modicum of conservative luggage plus golf clubs, guns or fishing rods in battered leather cases, and above all to seek out his advice on all subjects. He is the social arbiter of the guests and the vengeful scourge of the staff.

A case in point: descending early one morning to breakfast in one of the poshest hotels in Scotland, I stepped into the elevator, which was fully loaded with a mound of tartan luggage, an American tourist with guide book clutched in her hand, and a scrawny, red-polled bell-boy of, perhaps, fifteen. No sooner had the doors closed than the tourist cawed to the youngster: 'Tell me, young man, where can I find the Loch Ness monster?' The tone, the baggage, the guide book and the fact that the Loch Ness monster, if indeed it exists, dwells in the secret depths of a loch at least three hundred road miles away, rather than out in the pond below the rose garden, caused me to lower my eyes in humiliation on her behalf. The boy, himself covered with confusion at being addressed directly on such a weighty and unknown subject, and properly schooled in his hierarchical responsibilities, stared at his highly polished boots and mumbled, 'I dinna ken, ma'am. Ye'd best ask th' hall porter.' Then, proudly, 'He knows *everything!*'

Yes, he does know everything, the hall porter, that St Peter in wing collar.

There is only one way to get on with hall porters. When you arrive or when you leave for a morning's stroll or game of golf, simply say, 'Good morning.' Before retiring at night, pass by the front door, step out to inspect the sky and then seek out the superior intelligence of the hall porter. He will tell you precisely what kind of weather to expect on the morrow and, the B.B.C. to the contrary, you may bank on his opinion. You then thank him and bid him good-night. If you are interested in a county event, the departure of a train from Glasgow or the sailing of a steamer, he will take the matter under consideration and will, unfailingly, inform you next morning. If you are lonely and want to be

chummy, wait until the chief is having his tea or dinner and chat
to your heart's content with the under hall porter. Since he has
taken due note of your respect for the master and stands himself
in the need of a few kind words, he will be effusive to a high
degree.

There is one hall porter whom I have known – if that is the
correct word – for many years now and he has been of great help
to me in the many small matters I have set under his austere nose.
Our relationship has struck the right balance and I know that I
have played the game correctly and that I stand high in his august
opinion, since he never fails to address me in the third person.
Console yourself that you are beyond the pale if the hall porter
ever refers to you as 'you'. You're done, washed up. You've not
observed the rules. But, then, there are always other hall porters
and you can review your behaviour and start all over again with
an unblotted copybook.

16. The Groaning Board

IT IS considered quite worldly-wise to say 'British food is deplor-
able' and roll one's eyes either to heaven or toward the coast of
France. This may or may not be true of English cooking, but
Scottish cooking is another thing altogether. After all, you can get
a terrible meal any place in the world, even in your own home.

The Scots are fine bakers and pastry cooks. Their fish, game
and meats are excellently prepared. Their soups are pure
ambrosia. However, beware of hotel and restaurant vegetables
and bread sauce, the traditional accompaniment of domestic or
wild fowl, which I can only liken to library paste. I can't say anything laudatory about custards either, but you can always ask for
your tart or pudding without it. But that ends my criticisms. From
there on Scottish cookery is pure delight.

Take breakfast. Please do, in all its glory. Even if you're a coffee
and toast type at home make a point in Scotland of eating a good
Scottish breakfast. Don't worry about the calories. You'll walk
them off. And even if you don't you can always diet when you get
back home. Begin with juice or fruit. Then a good dish of porridge with country cream, then eggs (boiled are best, as you'll

discover for yourself), or Ayrshire bacon (which is rather like Canadian bacon), or kippers or kidneys. Better not try the sausage unless you're particularly fond of fried sawdust. Around the table will be set a rampart of crisp toast, a wonderful freshly baked breakfast roll called a 'bap', oatcakes, perhaps, and an assortment of jams, honey and marmalade. You will note that there's none of this bit of jam or jelly in a wee plastic container, but whole jars of the best brand available.

Now, what to drink? If you like tea, have it. Or hot chocolate. Or milk. As to the coffee, although I persist in drinking it, I have the impression that it is left over from the night before. The Scots brew excellent after-dinner coffee, so it follows that breakfast coffee ought to be of the same calibre. But, since the difference between the two is so marked and since the Scots loathe waste, I am convinced that the chef thriftily pushes the night's remains to the back of the cooking stove to await the next day's breakfast. This is the only possible explanation. Anyhow, you're among a nation of tea drinkers.

Lunch is another good meal, especially to be taken when sightseeing or travelling. It can be a heavy meal of, say, three courses; or, as I have mentioned before, a lovely cold plate of beef, chicken, ham, tongue and lamb accompanied by a garden salad. You could also choose cold salmon and mayonnaise. Now is the time for cider, beer or ale or an iced lager.

Tea should be taken about four or four-thirty to fill in the gap before dinner, which is latish. Tea becomes the big moment of the afternoon. There are several kinds of tea. The tea taken by one group of people who have had dinner at noon will make a gargantuan repast of everything from eggs to fish and (I hate to say it) spaghetti on toast. The other kind is for those who plan a hearty dinner. For this meal you will have, besides tea, sandwiches, fresh bread, scones (the 'o' pronounced like the 'o' in 'gone'), bannocks, tea pancakes, oatcakes, Dundee cake, short bread and French pastries. After this take a brisk walk and then lie down until it is time to dress for dinner.

At dinner, let yourself go. A Scots dinner goes on and on. Start with a very fine pâté, or smoked salmon, or assorted hors d'oeuvre. Then soup. Don't pass over the soup, because the Scots really understand the mysteries of the soup kettle. Then, fish.

Then, the entrée with vegetables, two kinds of potatoes followed by salad if you wish it – but I don't think you will. Dessert follows, and the whole affair is brought to a glorious close with a basket of tiny bonbons, cookies and sugared fruit. With dinner have wine: glass, carafe or bottle. Coffee is not included in the price of dinner and is not generally taken in the dining room, but in the lounge. Coffee, drunk *with* a meal, is unthinkable; and since it would probably come from that pot at the back of the stove and put in a large cup, it would also be undrinkable. However, coffee in the lounge, set out on a tiny table, is delicious. With it will be served a bowl of what will look like brown broken glass. These are called coffee crystals and have a faint taste of rum. If you take your coffee black, say so. If you need cream, ask for your coffee 'white'.

The Scots, as must be obvious, love to eat, and one has the impression that business and other such mundane pursuits are only something to do to fill in the time that lamentably exists between meals. The normal Scot has only four meals a day. There are others who manage to insert a little something about eleven o'clock in the morning, and for those who lean toward a heavy tea, a bit of supper and some tea before retiring.

Oh, yes, the Scots love to eat. And, with what they have to eat, I can't say that I blame them. Just contemplate salmon, trout, Aberdeen-Angus beef, lamb every bit as good as the French *pré-salé,* venison and grouse.

On menus not given over to French cuisine, but holding fast to Scottish cookery, you will find some dishes that may bear a bit of description and which I urge you to try in spite of some rather outlandish names.

Soups

Barley Broth – this is commonly called Scots Broth and is a meal in itself: lamb, peas, barley, cabbage, turnips and carrots. It is so thick that a spoon can stand upright in it, or at least ought to be able to.

Cock-a-Leekie – a tradition among Scots soups made of chicken, leeks, rice and, in the purest form, prunes. But don't let that put you off!

Partan Bree – a very rich soup made of crabmeat, anchovy paste and cream.

Cullen Skink – smoked haddock and potatoes share the honours in this soup with the horrendous name.

Hotch-Potch – a summer version of Scots broth but made with fresh young vegetables straight from the garden instead of barley and dried peas.

Main Dishes

Finnan Haddie (or *Findon Haddie*) – haddock in cream sauce served with potatoes, poached eggs or whipped cream.

Mince – ground beef, well seasoned, served with boiled potatoes.

Mince Pies – mince tucked inside pastry-lined muffin tins and baked brown. Lovely for a snack with beer.

Musselburgh Pie – thin strips of steak are wrapped about oysters, covered with beef broth and baked under a puff-paste crust.

Forfar Bridics – oval pieces of pastry, like small footballs (American style, that is) filled with steak and onions.

Scotch Eggs – hardboiled eggs, coated with sausage meat, rolled in crumbs and deep fried.

Vegetables

Stovies – potatoes cooked with butter and onion on top of the stove, i.e. in a frying pan.

Colcannon – potatoes and cabbage mixed together, sometimes sprinkled with cheese and browned in the oven.

Clapshot – mashed potatoes mixed with turnips, topped with chives. I ate tons of it as a child, and it's very good indeed.

Desserts

Flory, Prune or Apple – a pie made with dried fruits, thickened sauce and a pastry crust.

Scots Trifle – custard, sponge cake, jam, whipped cream, sherry and fruit.

Cranachan – whipped cream is mixed with toasted oatmeal plus a good dollop of whisky or rum.

Black Bun, Dundee Cake and Scottish Seed Cake – variations of fruit-cake, all delicious.

Grosset Fool – gooseberries and whipped cream, puréed.

These dishes plus the easily recognizeable salmon, grouse,

scones, bannocks, oatcakes, shortbread, venison and rabbit pies are only a small, representative sampling of Scottish fare.

I could go on, but instead, I'm going into the kitchen to look up a recipe for Devilled Beef Bones. I'm starving!

17. Gie's A Blaw

LISTENING to bagpipes is like eating snails. You are either transported with sheer joy or you are reduced to a state of quivering revulsion.

If you don't like bagpipes, you are not alone. You would undoubtedly agree with Tobias Smollett when he said, 'The sound of the Highland bagpipe . . . sings in the nose with a most alarming twang, and, indeed, is quite intolerable to the ears of common sensibility . . .' Should you feel that the music of the pipes is not musical at all, but as tuneless and aggravating as the caterwauling of a troop of tomcats on Saturday night, admit it at once. When confronted with a piper and his pipes, about to go into action, is no time for noble pretence, for the very expression on your face betrays the full extent of your apprehensive agony. Pipers are pretty sensitive too, and by no means can you throw a shoe at a piper as you would at a yowling tomcat. Your only recourse is a dignified escape from earshot, which has to be awfully far away, I assure you.

There is found in one single word the common denominator between 'liking' and 'not liking'. The word is 'skirl'. This is a much-used word, applied to the sound of the bagpipes. It means 'a loud, discordant sound' in Scots. Now, if you hate the pipes, a 'skirl of the pipes' sounds like a pretty apt description. To the enthusiast, a true connoisseur of pipe music, a 'skirl' is a clinker, a misplayed note on the chanter, a result of faulty fingering or letting the air pressure vary. So take your pick. A lot of pipers may disagree with me about this, but I cling to the Scottish dictionary and the word of the greatest piper in all of Scotland.

I myself have an absolute passion for the music of the pipes. In fact, I feel just the same way as did my esteemed and gentle grandmother, who confided in me, as an impressionable child, that if she had the pipes playing behind her and a gun in her hand she could shoot anyone.

Perhaps a summary information about bagpipes is indicated here for there is much about them that is not generally known. The bagpipe is an ancient instrument, known and used by the Moors and Arabs, and also played in Spain, Ireland, Germany and Greece, and the English County of Northumberland. The Scottish pipe was first known, or rather its use recorded in history, in the fourteenth century. The pipe played by many generations of Highlanders was, and is, the *Piob Mhor,* the Great Pipe. It differs from the Irish War Pipe only by the addition of a second tenor drone.

Interestingly enough, the bagpipe, like its ancestor the horn-pipe, is an indirectly blown instrument. It consists of several parts: the air is blown first through a wooden blow-pipe into a sheepskin bag. Pressure from the player's left arm moves the air through the reeds in the three drones and the chanter. The melody is played on the chanter, by covering and uncovering the holes with the fingers.

There are eight holes on the chanter, which allow nine tones, eight in the octave scale and one more. They are strangely tuned at intervals of High C to High D, and High F to High G. The notes are not exactly equal to the notes on a piano, although through the gradual sharpening of standard and concert pitch, the chanter's A is the B flat of the piano. In general, however, a piper friend of mine vows that none of the tones are sharp unless the piper has a tin ear, but then he is a true musical scholar, dedicated to the pipes. The big bass drone is thirty inches in length and the two tenor drones are half as long. All three are adjustable for tuning. The tenors are tuned an octave below the A of the chanter and the bass drone is tuned an octave below the tenors. The tenor drones are tuned to play in unison. These facts are not something that the visitor need have at his fingertips, but it is pleasant to have a little 'inside' information. You never know when it might come in handy, especially if accompanied by a suitably knowledgeable expression.

A bagpipe is not considered to be a nice little souvenir to bring back from Scotland, not, that is, unless you play the pipes and want a set from the source. Since the stocs (drones, chanter and blowpipe) are made of either imported African blackwood or cocoa wood, decorated with silver or ivory and the whole instrument lovingly made by hand, the bagpipe is quite expensive. A good set of pipes will cost from twenty-four pounds sterling to one hundred and ten pounds sterling, more or less. However, if you do play, it would be a fine investment, because a real piper would be able to try out all of the drones and the chanter before he bought a set. If you are musical at all, you might enjoy buying a practice chanter on which to learn the tunes. This is an especially good way to drown out your wife and annoy any over-tolerant neighbours whose children are addicted to pop music played at full decibel. A truce might be arranged.

The music of the pipes is divided into two types. The first is the *Piobaireachd* or *Ceòl Mor*. This is the great, ancient, classical music and is an expression of the heroic values of a world long gone, living only in passionate memory. The *Ceòl Mor* commences with a theme (the *urlar*) and variations governed by a strict set of rules. Then follows the *Taorluath,* and last, the *Crunluath* and variations on both. The whole *Piobaireachd* may end with a repetition of the first theme, the *urlar.* It all sounds very complex, and it *is.* Nevertheless, a devotee of jazz or Bach's improvisations would be utterly fascinated.

The second type of music for the pipes is the *Ceòl Aotrom,* which is the kind of music most people associate with the bagpipes. This is what is heard at the Edinburgh Tattoo and is played by pipe bands of military organizations and Scottish societies around the world. These are the marches, the reels, the strathspeys, the jigs and the hornpipes dear to the hearts of the Scots.

To those who are uninitiated in this great art form, let me say that the sound of the bagpipe is an expression of a heart leaping with joy or burdened with sorrow. This music is the very spirit, the pride of Scotland. It is history recorded in music, the jubilation of battle won, the lament for the fallen in a lost cause, a cry for vengeance, a salute to a hero, a march to stiffen the dedication of a soldier or, even, a dance at a country ball or a graceful tribute to a lady.

So important was the great Highland bagpipe to the spirit of the Scottish people that the government in London forbade its use, upon penalty of death, after the Rising of 1745 when the Stuart claim to the throne was finished forever at Culloden. This supposed 'weapon of war' was proscribed for an entire genera-

Old Bridge of Dee, Invercauld, Braemar

Loch Awe, Argyll

Balmoral Castle, Aberdeenshire

Weaver's Shop, Isle of Skye

tion of Scots. It was not until just before the Crimean War, a century later, that the pipe bands began to be formed and many of the most famous marches and airs date from that time. Ironically, it seems that a 'weapon of war' was deemed a good thing to lead stalwart Scottish regiments into battle for Queen, Country and Empire.

And, at last, one can again hear the great music of the mountains. One's blood is stirred as it was many centuries ago and strange visions come to the mind of the native Scots and those of Scottish descent and one is overcome with a feeling of joy or sorrow and, most of all, by a swelling pride.

> Pibroch of Donuil Dhu
>   Pibroch of Donuil
> Wake thy wild voice anew,
>   Summon Clan Conuil.
>
> Come away, come away,
>   Hark to the summons!
> Come in your war array
>   Gentles and commons.
>
> Come from deep glen, and
>   From mountain so rocky;
> The war pipe and pennon
>   Are at Inverlochy.
>
> Come away hill-plaid, and
>   True heart that wears one,
> Come every steel blade, and
>   Strong hand that bears one.

WALTER SCOTT

18. Garb Of Old Gaul

THERE IS one universal phrase in current American usage that is absolutely guaranteed to set my teeth on edge. Seemingly innocuous, but so vastly irritating to me and, I might add, to many others, are the words 'a plaid skirt'.

E

Almost every edition of the slick, chic fashion magazines in America, both in advertisements and photo copy, has the nasty, ignorant habit of using the word 'plaid' with dashing impunity. 'A plaid skirt!' The height or depth of redundancy! Let's not even stoop to discuss 'plaid' carpets or 'plaid' jackets. As to the 'plaid' necktie – forsooth. The wearer would suffocate.

Yet Americans, taking the lead from the fashion world, think they know what they mean when they toss the word around. They don't.

To set things straight, 'plaid' is not an adjective. It is a noun. Furthermore, it is pronounced 'played'.

A plaid is an article of clothing, which with one small exception, cannot be purchased as a garment. In the old days, a plaid was a length of material about two yards wide and four or six yards in length. This great swath of material was once loosely pleated about a man's waist and tightly belted. The long end that was left over was draped up over his shoulder and pinned securely with a brooch. The total effect was a sort of woolly toga. In the daytime, it was a highly suitable mode of dress; at night it served as a blanket. This original plaid was later adapted into the philabeg or, in modern language, the kilt. The pleats are now stitched and there is nothing to toss over the shoulder. However, for ceremonial occasions, for real purists and for pipers, there exists the 'fly plaid' which is a small, fringed shawl-like piece of material fastened to the shoulder and tucked under the belt behind. This is a remnant in more ways than one.

What the fashion editors and copywriters mean is one word, pure and simple, for the checkered or patterned material, traditionally woollen. The word is 'tartan'. A *tartan* skirt, a *tartan* tie. Let's not go any further. A tartan jacket or a tartan rug is too loathsome even to consider, although a tartan carpet has been unrolled at Prestwick Airport, for reasons known only to the airport's authorities.

Tartans with their distinctive patterns, called the sett, of various combinations of colours woven in different widths up and down, are never the same. They are the personal, individualized trademark of a certain clan and its septs, families bearing other names who belong through alliance or marriage to the parent clan. In this way, one look at the tartan of a man's kilt will tell at once who he is and, generally, where he is from.

Each clan tartan also has several distinct variations.

First, there is the standard clan tartan which is most generally worn. This is further divided into old colours, in which the colours are the same but seem faded, and softer than the bright regulation tartan.

Dress tartans were originally 'arisaids', tartans of the family design on a white background and worn by the women of the clan.

There are in some clans a black and white sett that was once used for mourning observances.

Hunting tartans are woven with a green, brown, purplish or grey background and they blend into the background of heather and bracken. If there is a choice in the matter, these are the tartans worn in the daytime, with the brighter ones saved for dress wear.

There are also two other tartans: the chief's tartan, reserved for his and his family's own use; and district tartans, very ancient, that are worn by people of a certain locality and may not belong to a clan. And remember that many, many Scots do not belong to a clan.

To be specific, I have four kilted skirts, each one in a different type of my family's clan tartan. I have a dress tartan in bright red, an 'old colours' dress tartan, muted down to the shade of tomato juice, an 'old colours' hunting tartan in soft green and blue, and a black and white sett. I also have a dinner skirt in the bright regulation hunting green. Freddie has the right to wear the tartan of two great clans and now that he has the complete range of kilts in tartans allowed by one clan, he has begun to work on the other. It gets to be rather expensive, but then, he wears Highland dress, plus Lowland trews, several times a week. Such a bird of paradise!

In the truest sense, a man or woman should have the 'right' to wear a certain tartan and those who do are very proud of that right, with justification. So, though no one would stop you from doing so, I would give the matter deep consideration before buying tartan. Women are the worst offenders because they generally select a tartan just because they think the colours are pretty. If you have the right, wear it with pride. If you don't, wear it with pleasure. The Balmoral tartan must never be worn, though, for it is solely for the use of the Royal family. The most commonly purchased tartan, which is even lamentably made up in luggage in America, is the Black Watch tartan. Through some quirk of history, the Black Watch (regimental) tartan is also the hunting tartan of one of Freddie's clans, but he doesn't have any interest in wearing it.

There are tartans that lovers of Scotland without a drop of Scottish blood may wear and feel no embarrassment. These are the Caledonian tartan and, if available, the Jacobite. There is even one for the clergy.

I'm being pretty arbitrary in this matter, but there is no point in the visitor being blissfully ignorant. The family tartan is a great source of pride to the Scot and torrents of blood have been spilled over them for many centuries. Hence, the clan tartan is not just a design. It is personal history and the man who wears his family's tartan can stand up straight and tall next to any other man, for he, and the world who sees him, knows who he is and what he represents.

And yet, in spite of everything, all of the rules and regulations, I would be most happy to ignore it all, if you would join me in an all-out effort to wipe the word 'plaid' from the American vocabulary.

19. Take One Sheep's Pluck

HAGGIS, the national dish, I suppose, of Scotland, is pronounced quite often to rhyme with 'ugh'. That is not how it tastes, just how some people pronounce it, 'huggis'.

There are many tiresome misconceptions about this dish. First, the Scots do not shovel it down at every meal. Once a dietary staple, it is now rather ceremonial in character, served on Saturday night at the big hotels for the benefit of foreign visitors who tremble in awful anticipation, or at Burns' Nicht Suppers throughout the world from Hong Kong to Buenos Aires. I rather imagine that the ceremonial part serves to remind the Scots, their visitors and those transplanted Caledonians how things have changed around Scotland. That remark can be taken any way you choose!

Secondly, haggis is no longer *necessarily* made from the stomach of a sheep, nor sheep's pluck (and never mind what *that* is), nor any other occult ingredients.

Thirdly, there was a very good reason for this use of animal oddments. The laird got the best cuts of the sheep, the chops or rack and the legs. It was, after all, his sheep. The others got what was left over and they blended it with another Scottish staple, oatmeal. To a shepherd or crofter down from the hills on a cold winter night of rain and snow and wind, it tasted very fine, indeed. To me, it still does.

Actually, haggis is not unlike the American's Philadelphia scrapple. It's just not fried. So, to those brave souls about to embark on their first spoonful of haggis, let me say that you will, most likely, be eating 'pot haggis', a sort of pudding made of nothing more frightening than chopped liver, minced heart, onions, toasted oats, marjoram, pepper and salt. It is generally served with 'bashit neeps' (mashed turnips) and a dash of whisky sprinkled over or sipped on the side.

And that is the pure, simple truth about haggis, 'Great chieftain o' the puddin' race.'

20. Widowed By A Guttie

AS ONE of those traditionally pitiful creatures known as golf widows (and there are many in our sisterhood), I can't find a great many delightful things to say about golf. That is, not usually. However, it does get me to Scotland in the summer. So therefore, I'm all for golf over *there*. At home, I just grin and bear it. We would probably go to Scotland regularly even if it weren't for the great golf to be had, but it does add a measure of excitement – what I really mean is hysteria – to Freddie's plans for the summer. You see, he won a quaich, a flat engraved cup, like a porringer, at St Andrews on our very first trip, and he's never been the same since. Unfortunately, he's like a tenor who hit the highest and purest note of his career on stage at the Lincoln Center and he keeps trying to repeat the performance. Alas, not with the same success. He did manage to shoot a 74 from the back tees of the Queen's Course at Gleneagles, which is a darned good score, and I would have been vicariously thrilled for him had he not leaned his score card against the water jug and stared at it raptly all through dinner, without a word to me except for a few sentences that contained the word 'birdie' and 'canned' with monotonous regularity. But that was all right, too, for I had the lavender and green Ochil hills in the twilight glow to gaze out upon and a slice of Tay salmon on my plate with Angus beef to follow. You see, Scotland does have its compensations for the golf widow!

One slight deviation, I feel is necessary here. A golf widow is a wife who is unselfish enough to let her husband play golf with his male friends and not 'take up the game' so they can play together. Unless a wife is a really good golfer, or the happiness of a husband depends upon having his wife beside him at all times, then I think men should be allowed their own game. Frankly, I feel terribly sorry for men who have to drag around the course every weekend, against their unspoken wishes, with their wives in tow, chirping away about bills and children's problems, paying little attention to their game and spading up huge divots of manicured grass. It's far better to let the men have a little time in the open air with the 'boys' and have relaxed and happy husbands return home. After all, if a woman really wants to play golf she can always find some other women to play with, and everyone is happy. However, I *choose* to remain a golf widow. I've never touched a club and I don't intend to do so. I am rapidly becoming a bit fed up with the twentieth century's feminine spirit of competition and 'beating men at their own game'. Let them alone – that's my policy.

Golf, pronounced 'gowf' or 'goff' in Scots, has been *the* game in Scotland since the fourteenth century. It is both national and democratic.

It is national in the sense of universality, because golf courses in Scotland are like sand-lot baseball diamonds in America: every small town and hamlet has one. Every place you go you'll find a golf course nearby and a real enthusiast could play a different course twice a day, every day, if his breath held out.

It is democratic in that all classes of society play, generally on the same courses. In 1770, my old friend Tobias Smollett said, 'Of this diversion the Scots are so fond that when the weather will permit, you may see a multitude of all ranks, from the senator of justice to the lowest tradesman, mingled together in their shirts. . . ' This, with the possible exception of a few private clubs, is still true, since most golf courses are municipal property open to all ratepayers. Two other reasons for the democratic aspect of the game is that a round of golf is very inexpensive and golf is, as every player knows, the great social leveller. An Earl who, though frightfully keen, plays like a gowk, can be easily put down by a coal miner who plays a scratch game on the same course.

Golf probably originated from Holland, where it was played on ice. Now, there's a thought! The golf balls were originally imported from Holland, but Scots thrift and long-headedness soon put a stop to this traffic and, seeing a good thing growing by leaps and bounds, began to make their own.

The first balls were of leather, filled with feathers. Then, balls called 'gutties', made of guttapercha, took the place of 'featheries'. Some bright soul discovered that the more nicks a ball had the farther and truer it went. So the makers began to put small indentations on them. Thus, today, we have that dimpled darling, the rubber-cored golf ball. By the way, there's a difference between British and American golf balls, and in Scotland the player must use British balls. The American golf ball is 1.68 inches in diameter and the British is 1.62 inches. For some strange reason they both weigh 1.62 ounces.

Back to history! The game of golf had its ups and downs in Scotland. It was played with mass enthusiasm until 1457, when the game was interrupted by James IV who decreed that 'Fute ball and golfe shall be utterly cryit downe and nocht usit.' His motive was that his subjects should pay less attention to swatting small balls around the dunes and give their undivided attention to perfecting their archery in order to win more battles against the English. James may have felt, and rightly, that the Scots could not successfully fight their unfriendly southern neighbours with golf balls; but he himself continued to play the game, as his official, financial records show regular expenditures for golf balls. But, after all, he was a king, not an archer. When the development of gunpowder exploded the whole practice of warfare, the Scotsmen were able to forget about the 'wapenshaws', the shows of arms, and get back to playing golf. It was then that the canny bowmakers, now anachronistic, turned their skilled hands to making golf clubs.

If Scots are accused today of being 'fitba-mad', then in those days, many centuries ago, the Scots could have been called 'gowf-mad'. Everyone got into the game. It was bruited about that even Queen Mary played a sporty round at Leith three days after the murder of her husband, Darnley. A fifteenth-century bishop of St Andrews got himself voluntarily and wholeheartedly involved in a successful effort to allow residents of St Andrews to play golf whenever they pleased on their town's course. The Calvinists tried to prevent golf being played on the Sabbath, but such was the pressure that was brought to bear on the church that the Sunday golfers were allowed to play anytime *except* when the sermon was being preached. Today, however, Sunday play is not allowed on certain courses and a guide book should be checked before starting out. The reasons may be religious and they may also be to protect the working man who can only play on Sunday, in which case it is only visitors who are denied access.

Scotland is pock-marked with golf courses, but some of them are world-famous. I would like to list a few, not actually in order of importance, except for the first.

1. *The Old Course, St Andrews.* Par 73. This is a 'town' course and all may play, but the club, the Royal and Ancient, which was founded in 1754, is closed to everyone except members and their guests. One gets a starting time by ballot which adds just that much more zestful chance to the course that has challenged the world. It is the R. and A. that frames the rules for the game and hands down decisions on disputes which are accepted as golf gospel all over the world, *except* in the United States.

2. *Muirfield.* This is the course of the Honourable Company of Edinburgh Golfers and was established in 1744. An introduction is essential to this, the oldest and most exclusive of clubs. I can find no par listed, but the records show a scratch score of 66 for a professional and 68 for an amateur.

3. *Carnoustie.* Par 74. This championship course or links belongs to the town and only has one restriction: an iron cannot be used from the tee. Here is to be found the infamous Barry Burn which must be crossed seven times during the progress of play.

4. *Royal Aberdeen Golfing Club.* (Par 72). An introduction is needed to this club, which was founded in 1780.

5. *Rosemount.* (Par 75). This course at Blairgowrie was designed by the great James Braid.

6. *Gleneagles.* (King's Course Scratch 71 and Queen's Course Scratch 69). Both of these courses are more of Braid's genius and offer grandiose and luxurious golf.

7. *Machrihanish.* (Par 70). This is a difficult course to get to, since it is located near Campbeltown on Kintyre, but it is one of the best.

8. *Prestwick Golf Club.* (Par 72). An introduction is necessary to this historic club, which has played a leading part in the development of the modern game of golf.

9. *Troon Old Course Golf Club.* (Par 74). With Prestwick, the 'old and classy', this open championship links has no restrictions, but a reserved starting time is a good idea for week-end play.

10. *Turnberry.* (Ailsa Course and Arran Course, Par 73). The twin seaside courses were designed by MacKenzie Ross, and after that little need be said to commend them.

11. *Royal Dornoch.* (Par 72). This course lies far to the north in Scotland but is well worth the trip to visit it.

There are many more fine clubs and courses, especially in the suburbs of Edinburgh and Glasgow and in the southern part of Scotland. The above are called 'Freddie's Favourites' or 'Freddie's Nemeses', as the mood after a skirmish strikes him. A brochure listing the other good courses can be obtained by writing to the British Tourist Association at 680 Fifth Avenue in New York or by calling at the Scottish Tourist Board at 2 Rutland Place in Edinburgh. You may easily map your battle plan from the booklet.

Some of of the holes on the above mentioned courses have wondrous and often damnably descriptive names: Pint Stoup (a measure of ale or other liquor which you'll probably need), Needle E'e (Eye), Risk an' Hope, Dinna Fouter (Don't Bungle), and Woe Betide. There is a bunker at St Andrews Old Course aptly named Hell.

There are several more joys to playing golf in Scotland in addition to the Elysian fields themselves. The first are the starters who get the players off ON TIME! The second are the rangers who keep people moving, and through their firm tact prevent a round of golf from becoming a nature ramble. This is why golf widows are quite content in Scotland. A game can be played in the morning and still leave time for a leisurely lunch and a sightseeing jaunt in the afternoon. The ranger is the golf widow's friend. The third and last reason, are the caddies. Originally, a caddie was an errand boy in Scottish cities, a trusty messenger. The word comes from 'cadet' meaning young, but some of today's 'young' fellows are pretty long in the tooth. They know the game and they are intimately acquainted with every blade of grass or clump of whins on the course. So don't be surprised if he wanders off to look for a bird's nest to see if the 'wee bairns' are out of the egg yet. He knows where the nest is and he also knows *just* where your ball is. If he should suggest a club to use, take his advice. And if he tells you to 'hit it on pun, sir', he means the pin.

For a golfing widow, I've learnt a lot!

21. Pardon Me, Your Knees Are Showing

IF YOU come to Scotland expecting to see all of the male natives dressed like the late Harry Lauder, you're in for a surprise.

Highland dress is not generally worn, for several reasons. First, tartan, kilt and bagpipes were proscribed on pain of death or transportation to the colonies or prison after the '45 and the battle of Culloden. The crown, the one in London, that is, felt that tartan and bagpipes were inflammatory to an already fiery people. Match to the tinder, so to speak.

However, this proscription didn't last too long, for it was repealed in 1785. The act was shameful on the face of it, but the really pitiful part was that in forty years the old patterns of the tartans were lost, the weavers had passed away and, worse, the Highlanders had got used to trousers. There was a tartan revival, begun amusingly enough by George IV, great-grandson of George II who had been king in 1745, and was made even more popular by Queen Victoria and Prince Albert. It must be admitted though that the last two went rather overboard about it and the whole matter reeked of Germanic sentimentality. It became *de rigueur* with the court, the English visitors 'up for the season' and the anglicized Scottish upper class (an English term, not a Scots) to be decked out in everything but the kitchen sink in the way of Highland dress. The Scottish costume of the Victorians was a travesty upon the manly and practical garb of old Gaul, *sic Gael.*

A second deterrent to the more universal use of the kilt is a matter of money. The whole wardrobe, and wardrobe it *is,* is frightfully expensive. Granted it lasts for ever and needs little if any care, but the total cost is rather beyond the means of the average Scot, i.e. the Scot whose forefathers wore the kilt. There is a movement afoot to bring back this national dress, but I don't think with the swift movement of city life and the even swifter passage of money through the hands of the average man that the movement will spread like wildfire.

There are people who do wear the kilt, and often. There are also people who wear it mainly to evening affairs such as balls and receptions. The best chance for the visitor to see it on the private citizen, as opposed to military bands and the chance regiment on guard at Edinburgh Castle who still wear the kilt, is at Highland games.

There are two types of Highland dress, day and evening, and the components are quite different. This is where it gets expensive, as Freddie knows from unregretted experience.

Daytime dress consists of a kilt, generally in the hunting colours. This is topped with a short tweed jacket with wide cuffs, shoulder straps and horn or leather buttons. Underneath there is a matching tweed vest or weskit. With this is worn a white, green or tan shirt and a plain tie, *not* tartan. Hanging from a strap and chain from the waist is a brown leather sporran, with or without tassels. A sporran is most necessary because a kilt has no pockets. Stockings of green or tan or blue wool, with garter flashes, or tabs of red or green, plus heavy brogans cover the lower part of the leg. The knee cap is left flagrantly exposed. In the top of the right or left stocking, depending upon whether the man is right or left handed, so as to be quick on the draw, is a horn handled knife in a scabbard, the *sgian-dubh* or *skean dhu.* There is a pin, safety or ornamented, with Celtic design or a grouse claw, at the lower right hand corner of the apron, which is what the plain front of a kilt is called. The pin is purely decorative and does not go all the way through to attach to the under-apron.

On his head the Scotsman wears a bonnet, locally pronounced

'bunnit'. This is generally dark blue with a red pom-pom called a tourie. It can also be light green or tan with a matching tourie. The bonnet is held tight with a ribbon whose ends are tied in a small bow or left hanging loose. There are several schools of thought. There are three kinds of headgear, the Balmoral, which is the most common, the Kilmarnock, and that leftover of the Victorians, the Glengarry. It is the Balmoral to which I refer. On the left side is pinned the wearer's clan crest within a 'strap and buckle', if he is not a chief. The chief wears the crest alone, plus one to three feathers according to his rank within the family clan.

In the evening, the Scotsman really becomes a bird of paradise, the term I have applied to my husband, for full Highland evening dress has no match in the entire world. In fact, when Freddie is forced by circumstances to wear normal black-tie dinner jacket, his whole personality changes.

First, the man wraps around his middle his best dress kilt. Then comes his first problem. He has a choice of jackets. He may wear either a short black jacket of velvet or fine wool, with silk lapels, the cuffs flapped and decorated with silver Celtic-design buttons and, most often seen, with short tails hanging down at the back and sides and ornamented with matching silver buttons. The vest, also black, is buttoned with silver. With this he generally wears a white shirt and black bow tie. His other choice is a doublet of black wool or coloured velvet to blend with the kilt, rich red, blue or green, fastened at the neck with silver buttons. At the neck is a lace jabot, and lace froths at his wrists. The doublet, being short, in front at least, is belted with a wide black leather belt and a large, rectangular silver buckle. Evening stockings are diced (chequered in red, *never* green unless they are pipers), full tartan design (like the American argyll socks but long), or plain with tartan cuffs. On his feet he wears black ghillies, long laces tied about his ankles, or a strapped shoe rather like a Mary Jane pump, with a silver buckle at the instep. In his stocking he wears a dress *skean dhu*, the handle of carved black wood and set with a cairngorm. For evening wear the silver trimmed sporran is made of fur, usually sealskin, with silver mounted tassels.

Naturally, it takes hours for a man to dress and for a change it is the wife who sits by tapping her foot or acting as valet. And even when he is all dressed and standing before you in his splendour, you both have the feeling that he has forgotten to put something on.

To answer the age-old question of what does a Scotsman wear under his kilt, I must give you two replies. Something or nothing, depending upon the preference of the wearer. If something is worn, it is short, tight cotton underpants dyed green. So now you know!

Now as to the length of the kilt. Americans, for some reason, have a tendency to wear the kilt too long. This is known as 'choking the knees' and is a bit womanish. Actually, to look best, and providing the man has decent legs, and most do, the kilt should end just above the knee-cap and it should not droop behind. The stockings should not be worn too high. The lower they are the better the effect. One inch or two below the knee is excellent. This is about the only time that the male kneecap is so appealing as to be made prominent.

Ladies are allowed none of this glamour, but we do have our small traditions. Ladies do *not* wear the kilt. They wear a pleated skirt of tartan or a 'kilted' skirt. The idea is the same but it is made with fewer pleats and is worn longer. It is to be hoped that the mini-kilt craze will soon be over! The rule is that the ladies' skirt should just clear the floor when the wearer kneels down.

In the evening, when Highland dress is in order, the lady wears a gown of plain material and over her shoulder is draped a silk tartan sash, pinned at the waist or shoulder with a Celtic brooch. There are a variety of ways of wearing the sash, all established by tradition, to indicate whether the wearer is a clanswoman, the wife of a chief or a woman who has married out of her clan and into another. The Lord Lyon King at Arms has tried to establish rules, but ladies being temperamentally what they are wear their sashes as they feel they are most becoming. Ladies often have dinner skirts made of wool tartan worn with a white blouse, which makes a charming costume for less formal evenings and is in no way objectionable.

However, we, puir lassies, have little choice compared with our men-folk.

22. Only On Weekdays

A DRUGSTORE in Scotland is called a dispensing chemist, and you can buy almost everything there you could buy in an American drugstore. In the big cities, there is always one of the large chain chemists open all night. But, for goodness' sake, if on Saturday night you find yourself out of hairspray or shaving cream, get it then! If you don't, you'll be hairy Neanderthals until Monday morning. Scotland has a set of very rigid laws that prevents a drugstore from selling *anything* except medicine and first aid supplies on Sunday. In fact, steel grilles keep you at a respectful but frustrating distance from all of the goodies on the well-stocked shelves, while the chemist doles out packets of pills at the dispensing counter. And all day Sunday your eager hands can reach out to, but never touch, as in a nightmare, the hairspray and shaving cream that would keep you from looking like a witch or a castaway.

And why is this all true? I'll bet you didn't know that film and deodorant and toothbrushes and combs were sinful, did you? Well, they are, according to the Scottish laws.

I wonder though if they'll let you buy paper tissues? I've never tried, but they would come in very handy for drying one's eyes before going to the kirk and hearing a nice long sermon about the evil, sinful temptations besetting the world. Things like hairspray and shaving cream, for instance.

23. 'L'

AS EVERY English-speaking child knows, A stands for Apple, B stands for Boy and so on. L stands for Lamb or Lion according to the nature of the child. But in Britain, to adults, L stands for something quite different. As you travel about the country, or in cities for that matter, you will see a plaque, riveted, bolted, wired or tied with a bit of string on cars, motor bikes and even trucks. In this case L stands for Learner. According to law, those people who have not passed their driver's tests must bear this awful red L on the vehicle every time they are behind the wheel. It doesn't always mean they are learning to drive. It means they don't know enough to pass the test. They are not adolescents, either, being painstakingly instructed by an adult. You'll be shocked to notice that some of them are grey-haired old veterans of the road. You'll be further shocked when you see an L on the rear of a very large truck making deliveries for a reputable firm. I've never yet seen one on a double-decker bus, but I'm waiting.

Now, the L has two meanings. First, the driver is not a good driver. That much is quite obvious, especially when a motor bike zooms past you into the teeth of heavy traffic with the senseless courage of Don Quixote. Believe me, it is an unnerving experience.

But secondly, and more important, it is a warning to other drivers to be prepared for *anything* and to give the vehicle with the red stigma a wide berth. In this instance, L really stands for 'LOOK OUT!'

Don't say I didn't warn you!

24. Who Is Nessie, Where Is He?

VISITORS to Scotland are always curious about the Loch Ness monster. Does it really exist, they want to know? There have been some pretty lively reports about divers who have gone down into the lake and vowed never to repeat the experience, meanwhile keeping a deathly silence on what they saw. Bodies, drowned in the lake, sometimes cannot be found. Stories like this can naturally give rise to a lot of wild talk.

The alleged monster is said to abide in the second largest fresh water lake in Scotland, twenty-four miles long and an awesome 754 feet deep. On the western shore stands the stark ruin of Urquhart Castle, which was besieged by Edward I in the fourteenth century. In its dungeon there is supposed to be a vault containing a vast treasure. The vault is also supposed to contain the plague. And all about are the mountains and dark glens where cattle raiders were beheaded, where Prince Charles Edward was hunted down like a wild beast after Culloden and where there occurred other black deeds of revenge which have been recorded in clan histories. Isn't that just the perfect setting for a monster? The whole plot called for – no, *screamed* for – a monster. Nothing less could possibly do – and if one could believe in treasure guarded by plague, why not accept the possibility that a monster lurks in the bottom of the lake?

I'm not about to say whether Nessie exists or not. I've never seen him, her or it. Some fairly reliable people have, though. The monster was first recorded in 565 when St Columba, at the moment engaged in preaching a sermon to the Picts, allowed his attention to stray to the lake and there was Nessie. Naturally, he took note of the fact immediately. Converting heathen Picts was one thing; monsters he had not bargained for when he left the Christian shores of Ireland.

Nessie has also been seen by numerous residents of the area from Fort Augustus to Lochend. Not all of them have been generations of locals weaving home of a Saturday night from the local pub or hillside *clachan*. The good monks at the abbey in Fort Augustus have seen the monster, too, as they went about their tasks. The 'tasks' that they were going about rather bother me because they are Benedictines and we all know what *they* make. This is just an idle thought and is in no way intended to be a reflection upon the integrity and sobriety of the monks.

It's rather too bad, in the interests of Scottish tourism, that science has to rear its ugly head instead of letting Nessie continue to rear its own head out of the murky water. But, no, there are those determined people who simply must blast a legend. While we're not sure about Nessie, there actually exists a Loch Ness Phenomena Investigation Bureau. The L.N.P.I.B. (I refuse to repeat or dignify the name of the group) has set up a command post on the shore of the lake – at a respectable distance, I might add – and has had the surface of the water under day and night surveillance, with cameras and other advanced recording equipment. They have also added a sonar- and radar-equipped submarine to their arsenal. I must say I do agree with Brigadier Simon Fraser, Lord Lovat, Chief of the Clan Fraser, and famed commando leader, in his feeling that scientific identification is one thing, but, to use his word, 'bullying' puir auld Nessie is going a bit too far. Perhaps the animal needs a Loch Ness Monster Protection Society. The L.N.M.P.S., as opposed to the L.N.P.I.B., would act in the interests of preserving a legend that has given pleasurable thrills of apprehension to thousands of visitors to that region. Take away Nessie and what have you got left? Just another lake. I don't notice any investigation bureau opening the plague vault at Urquhart Castle.

To get back to the original question. Does the animal really exist? I don't know. Unless I've been eye-ball to eye-ball with a monster, I never *am* completely certain of its existence. I mean, I know a monster when I see one and I haven't seen the Loch Ness Monster. This is neither here nor there. There are those who swear that they have seen it. There are documented photographs, grey and lumpy, of the monster as it swam on the surface of the lake at night. This may be convincing evidence. And, don't forget, the L.N.P.I.B. is on the alert.

For myself, I don't really want to know. I don't even want to see Nessie. I just want to believe that at the bottom of Loch Ness is a prehistoric animal. I like my scalp to tingle once in a while. I'm fed up with scientific answers to *everything*!

25. The Gaelic Carnival

IF YOU should find yourself up in the Highlands or in Edinburgh or Glasgow with a car at your disposal, during the summer or early autumn, there is a 'Happening' you must not miss if the opportunity arises. A three-ring circus is nothing in comparison!

This 'Happening' is really a loose term that covers three types of events, all first-cousins.

The first, and certainly the most glamorous, are the great Highland gatherings. Here is pomp and ceremony, often attended by royalty, where music and games and dancing are at their finest. It is so well done as to appear to be a rehearsed spectacle. The most famous of these is the Braemar Gathering, held in September when Her Majesty is in residence at Balmoral.

The second are the Highland games on a smaller scale. These are more of a local nature and are more appealing because they seem spontaneous.

The third is the agricultural fair or show and amateur sports meeting. Even more indigenous, these to me are the best of the lot and I wouldn't miss the Atholl and Breadalbane show at Aberfeldy, held each August, for all of the tea in China.

F

These affairs are really a modern translation of the old clan gatherings, the time when the families held their reunions, when clan business was discussed, the men pitted their physical strength against other family members, and young and old danced to pipe and fiddle. Now, new sports events have been added, the young people compete in exhibition Highland dancing, and flower displays and baking competitions take the place of clan business. Although some clans use these events as a chance to get together over luncheon in a special tent or marquee set up for the occasion, it is not purely 'family' now, but, rather, an event for everyone in the neighbouring countryside, with pipe bands coming from the big cities to entertain. And entertaining it all is.

The agricultural show is an added attraction. The farmers' very finest horses, cattle and sheep are loaded on trucks and brought out of the surrounding hills or up from the glens to the fair, where they are judged keenly by learned men who tag the prize specimens with blue, red and white ribbons. Then the animals are left in their pens for all to see, to be gloated over or argued about, as the case may be.

It is also a time for a few nips from the bottle, so the uneasy decorum of the morning soon fades into a general joviality as the afternoon progresses. About tea time, the livestock is loaded back on to the trucks, mothers gather up their children, wives seek out errant husbands, and off they go back to their farms after a day they will talk over during the long winter evenings.

If you should go to a game or fair, I suggest that you arrive about noon. You may bring a packed lunch from your hotel, or obtain modest refreshment from one of the tents set up by catering firms. The best on the menu here are meat pies and beer. I hold out for the packed lunch because you can find a bench or a spot under a tree and watch the goings-on while you eat. Besides, the hotel packed lunches are very, very good. Be sure to have them put in some bottles of lager and, lest I sound alcoholic, a thermos of tea.

Between one and four o'clock, prepare to enjoy yourselves enormously. Also, be prepared for rain and bring raincoats and umbrellas – one just never knows. If it's an agricultural show you're attending, wear rubber soled comfortable shoes for obvious reasons. I rather like 'muckin' boots', but few European travellers include such practical rubber footwear in their forty-four pounds air allowance. However, you'll be all right if, as the Scots say, you 'Gang warily'.

There's very little point in getting seats in the enclosure. All this means is a hard wooden chair to perch on, limited vision and the honour of the company of a 'county' lady, in flowered hat or voile toque, who will award the medals. We prefer to purchase general admission tickets to the grounds and wander about. There's so much to see!

First, there's people-watching – and just in case this gives you a slightly superior feeling, don't forget that they're watching *you*, too! You've not wandered into 'Brigadoon' (Broadway's spelling, not mine), remember. You'll see a complete cross-section of the very democratic Scottish society: chiefs and chieftains in Highland day dress, complete with cock feathers in their bonnets, their badge of office; county nobility; lairds; farmers and their robust families; old ladies done up to their chins in woollies; old men in ancient tweeds. There will also be a sprinkling of English visitors and a shower of tourists from America and the Continent, especially Germans. Try to be courteous and helpful. Offer your seat on a bench, if you have one, to an old lady, don't step on the dogs that race about underfoot, and cough understandingly at the antics of the local inebriate if he appears, and he *will*. Do try to locate the parents of lost small boys, kilted and sobbing, that you may encounter. With great regularity, the voice of the master or assistant mistress of ceremonies announces the disappearance of Hamish or Colin and the present location of his parents.

Speaking of the voices on loud-speakers, they are of two distinct kinds, both highly diverting. There is the master of ceremonies who invariably has a trenchant sense of humour and his comments throughout the afternoon are worthy of a professional comedian. The other, is his female counterpart who replaces him occasionally, especially to announce the winners of the flower arrangement and jam awards, and, possibly the dance competitions. Without fail, these worthy ladies, with their normally high-pitched British voices, become panic-stricken when coming face to face with a microphone, combined with a list that invariably becomes jumbled, and female hysteria takes over. They become rather incoherent as the afternoon wears on and their vocal pitch becomes higher and higher. I often wonder if they retire to the local hydropathic hotel for a jolly good rest when the day is over.

And now, to the main event, the general, semi-organized (in so far as the directors and convenors planned it) programme. The field is in a positive furore of activity and one scarcely knows where to look from one minute to the next.

In the main events field, enclosed by wire or rope there will first be a high wooden platform. On it and clustered about it are young people competing for medals in Highland dancing: reels, sword dance, fling, Sean Triubhas (meaning 'without trousers'), and Reel of Tulloch. A piper, generally of greatly advanced years, his face the texture and hue of a walnut, plays indefatigably for hours on end. Just beyond, burly men are lining up for the 'Heavy Events', tossing the sheaf, putting the 16- and 28-pound weight, throwing the 16- and 22-pound hammer and throwing the 56-pound weight over a high bar. The latter event is great fun, especially when the weight flies off the handle. We saw it happen once, with appropriate remarks upon the occasion from the master of ceremonies, as the competitor sprawled backwards on the muddy ground, his kilt flying awry, his face a mask of shock, until he, too, began to howl with laughter. In yet another open space, men are stripping down to singlets and kilts to toss the caber, a length of tree like a telephone pole, which must be thrown exactly end over end to land neatly on one end before it topples as straight and as far away as possible. This is not something to be bungled and loud are the groans that accompany a bad toss. At the far side of the field (and this is where I always lose Freddie) pipe judges listen solemnly to an equally solemn piper playing his best pibrochs, marches, reels and strathspeys as he passes back and forth in as stately a manner as possible on a tiny dais. This is a terribly serious business, since a good deal of prize money and piping medals are involved, to say nothing of a man's reputation in this difficult art. Within seemingly dangerous proximity to the caber tossing and weight putting, another group of giants, stripped to the waist, are slamming each other to the ground in catch-as-catch-can and Cumberland style wrestling.

And all about, in a dizzying ring, are the foot-racers, hill-racers, dashers, bicycle-racers and infant sack-racers, while the high-jumpers and the pole-vaulters leap and swing in the air, a Maypole in centre field about which all revolves in organized frenzy.

At certain games young ladies bring their prize horses and put them through their paces, or dress themselves and their mounts in allegorical costumes, although Lady Godiva has yet to appear – so don't be too hopeful on *that* score.

Suddenly, in the middle of this Scoto-Roman carnival, a police or military band marches out on to the field and the high point of the programme has been reached. Their presence does nothing to lessen the general activity. The pipers pipe on and the dancers dance on, but the martial music does manage to drown out the enraged bellows of the incarcerated bulls on the far side of the field.

I would suggest a tour of the cattle and sheep pens as the final event of your day, if this happens to be an agricultural show you are attending. Be certain to admire the winners with some show of knowledgeable but reserved interest, even if feigned. And don't make unkind remarks about the losers. The owners of both may be listening and fisticuffs may break out between them. At the very least, you yourself will be treated to a few terse words, fortunately none of which will be intelligible to you. The best approach is to look terribly keen and to be very, very quiet. Murmur something innocuous to your companion and move on.

Another word to the wise: when loading time comes absent yourself from the scene. I made the lamentable mistake one day of standing too close to a sheep van while a particularly recalcitrant ram was being urged up the ramp, in what to me, city female that I am, was a unique manner. Such was my pop-eyed fascination that I did not notice that the ramp was about to be slammed shut on the indignant beast and in a moment I disappeared in a shower of dry hailstones. Freddie offered to keep all the car windows open on the way home despite a temperature in the doleful forties. Since then I have learnt to keep a respectful distance from the loading of sheep, no matter how intriguing the bucolic performance.

If you can manage to attend one of these gatherings, it may well prove to be one of the happiest days of your life, especially if you come from a hectic city back home. You will have seen how the

Scots enjoy their life and share it with others. I hope it will be a day that you, too, will talk about occasionally on a long winter evening.

26. Blood On The Snow

THERE ARE two great 'crimes' in Scottish history, about which thousands of reams of paper have been written and opinions hurled, sometimes rather vehemently, back and forth, pro and con. They are both enigmas to intrigue the student of criminology. Even there, I go rather far. But facts are facts, if historians ever get them straightened out. The first is whether or not the beautiful Mary Stuart was a wicked, murderous queen, well tutored by the de Guise and the Medici at the French court, or a complete innocent, lied-about and led astray by others who were willing to make her a pawn in their political chess game. Frankly, I think the truth will forever be lost to us, despite the splendid work of historians who are fascinated by this young, tragic figure.

The second crime, if you will, is the Glencoe massacre. Here, the answers lie cruelly naked for all to see, if they wish to do so. However, there are fierce partisans for both sides and many, many factors enter into the story, so as to make the issue more complex than it appears. In fact, the disaster was a national one, the product of the age. In a way, Glencoe is not unlike a Greek drama in which the outcome is preordained. Once the events and situations leading to the crime were set into motion, there could be no turning back until destiny or the gods decreed the final tragic ending. Sometimes, I think that the Glencoe massacre wasn't all that horrible. Similar dark deeds happened many times before in both Scottish and English history, but Glencoe became a national issue, highly political, with even the King involved. So, perhaps, it has been blown-up out of all proportion.

To the average tourist, if he thinks about it at all, Glencoe is the place where the Campbells murdered the MacDonalds. That's what happened, all right, but it's not quite that simple.

So, for a deeper insight into the event, let's go back. To begin, we must look at the clan system. A discussion on the clans could go on forever, but a few facts will clear the air a bit. For centuries, secure in the Highland fastness created by nature and the hand of God, the great clans, their cadet branches, their allied clans and their septs (those families bearing allegiance to the chief of a greater clan), were a law unto themselves. Even the loyalties of the smaller groups and the alliances of the more powerful families shifted from time to time, friends one day, blood enemies the next. The pendulum swung crazily between *esprit de corps* to vendetta. One never really knew what went on in the hearts and minds of the clan chiefs and chieftains. Edinburgh was not always certain, and London hadn't a clue. Again, the reason was the Highland Line, the mountains themselves and an utter lack of rapid communication. The roads of the time were drovers' roads, over which cattle were driven to market, or sheep paths winding through the passes. It was not until General George Wade began constructing roads and bridges in the Highlands, between 1725 and 1736, or thereabouts, that the first real crack was made in the Highland *festung* and communication became somewhat more expeditious. Mind you, this rapidity cannot be compared to the speed of lightning, since there were only two-hundred and fifty miles of Wade's roads and transportation depended upon ponies and horses or a pair of sturdy legs.

The next factor was clan warfare itself. This was the old 'eye for an eye' philosophy carried out with appalling dispatch. Life in the mountains on a day-to-day basis was cruel in itself, and survival depended upon the utmost cunning and opportunism. Cattle were the major commodity of value and to steal its cattle was the quickest means of reducing a powerful rival clan to destitution. Murder, if murder were necessary to the act of stealing livestock, was merely incidental. Often the reasons for such rapine were trivial (at least, to us); but for the most casual of insults to a great family, the retribution far exceeded the cause. There was justice, of course, and magistrates and gaols, but these hardly mattered to the chiefs, who imposed their own laws and meted out their own justice. It was not that the chiefs and chieftains were barbarous. They had to protect their dependent feudal families, their lands, their castles, their goods and chattels, and they were not unmindful of the law. It was just that the law of the rocky passes, high in the clouds and blizzards, could not in any way be equated with the alien law of London as exercised in peaceful English villages.

Now we come to the political elements. On the whole, the High-landers rather preferred a Scottish king on the throne, and the exile of James VII (II of England) in favour of William of Orange and James' daughter, Mary, did not please them at all. Their loyalties (in spite of some lapses) to the Stuarts ran deep and religion was a profound motivation. Calvinism had not pene-trated very far into the hills and the Roman Catholics in the High-lands dreaded a 'killing time' just for the sake of a Protestant king. They also felt, as individuals, that they really owed allegiance to no outsider, crown or no crown. Loyalty was to the clan and its head, and that was that. A simple philosophy, unfortunately out-moded even then, and a great threat aimed at the absolute power of the Crown and an even greater threat to certain other Scots.

These 'certain other Scots' were the real troublemakers, the fly in the Highlander's porridge. Some of the more powerful Scots nobles, some clan chiefs, others not, saw *more* power within easy reach if they played along with London's schemes for the submis-sion of the Highlanders to the Crown. These were greedy men and their prize for treachery was predominance, position at Court, land and money. Actually, their crimes were far worse than any the Highland chiefs could ever evolve. They were devi-ous and felt bound by no rules. The Highlanders at least had a sense of honour, even if among thieves, and there were unwritten laws that contained some elements of gallantry. One of these laws was violated at Glencoe, and perhaps this was considered by them to be the most heinous fact of the crime.

And so we come to the year 1691, when it was decreed that all Highland chiefs and chieftains would swear an oath of fealty to William. London didn't give them much time: August 1691 until 1 January 1692, less than four months. Considering communica-tion, clan pride, interwoven alliances, gatherings for conferences, fears and stubbornness, this was difficult almost to the point of impossibility. For those clans close to the Highland line and those more realistic and tractable chiefs, the time was sufficient and they signed the necessary papers. They were near enough to Edin-burgh and the Lowlands to realize the determination of the gov-ernment and to recognize the terrible punishment that would be unleashed upon them if they did not submit at once. 'Letters of Fire and Sword' were to be issued against all who did not take the oath, and in view of the consequences, it was better to give a little to keep what they had. But in the mountains to the north, great parleys took place, many clans together, and the outcome was 'I will if you will'.

By December, most of the clans had taken the oath before the King's magistrate and had received the promise of indemnity. The last one to submit before the deadline was the Cameron of Lochiel, who travelled to Inverary and took the oath on 30 December 1691, just before the axe was to fall. There was only one left, one hold-out against His Majesty's law: old Alasdair MacDonald of Glencoe, chief of the clan of *Iain Abrach*. MacIain, as he was called, had been educated in France, but he was 'proudful' and his hatred of the Clan Campbell was intense. It was this hatred that was to be his downfall.

The chief of the Clan Campbell was Archibald Campbell, Earl, and later Duke, of Argyll. It was he who had offered the Scottish crown to William, but it was not a gracious, altruistic gesture. In return, he received the forfeited lands of his father, the ninth Earl, who had been beheaded by James VII for treason. Argyll had as little love for MacIain as the old MacDonald had for him. There had been the matter of the raids of the Glencoe men upon Inverary, the stronghold of the Campbells of Argyll, and upon the powerful Breadalbane and Glenlyon, Argyll's cousins. These were not to be taken lightly. Cattle were lifted by the Glencoe clan from other Campbell chieftains and this did nothing to improve the relationship either. So, when the opportunity presented itself, Argyll saw retribution and loyalty to the Crown all wrapped up in one neat package. In fact, as early as 1689, Argyll seized his opportunity to become the strong man of the Highlands by obtaining royal permission to raise what was to be known as Argyll's Regiment of Foot. It had the distinction of being the first British regiment to be raised in Scotland, and Argyll's little army pleased him mightily. So, MacDonald of Glencoe had his pride and Campbell of Argyll had royal favour and a fully armed regiment, and both of them shared a mutual hatred. The feud, though, had got out of balance and was exceedingly dangerous – to MacIain.

And what of Glencoe, the scene of the tragedy? Even by seventeenth century standards, it was remote. By today's standards, it is merely a few hours drive from Glasgow. To the north of gentle Loch Lomond, west of Rannoch Moor and south of Loch Leven, it is a short, rather sinister valley, about eight miles in length, twisting and turning through menacing mountains. It is, in one word, eerie. It has been called an enclosed garden, but that was some time ago. I rather tend to agree with Lord Macaulay who said, 'in an age of violence and rapine, the wilderness itself was valued on account of the shelter it afforded to the plunderer and his plunder.' This seems to me to be an exact description of the MacDonalds and their stronghold of Glencoe. Macaulay also called it the 'very Valley of the Shadow of Death'. I would call it a graveyard, unconsecrated, with no markers for those who died there. But, then, I am sentimentalizing – and for one very good reason: the law of the Highlands that was broken there.

On the night of 30 December, old MacIain, bent but unbroken, gave in at last and fought his way through a snowstorm, across Loch Leven and up to His Majesty's garrison at Fort William, over ten miles on foot along a rough road from Ballachulish Ferry, as it is now called. He presented himself to Colonel John Hill, governor of the fort. He asked to take the oath. Colonel Hill had to inform him that it was not he who could receive the allegiance, but the sheriff, who was then in Inverary. A Campbell sheriff, an enemy, was the man to whom MacIain must bow his head in submission. There was no other way. He must go to Argyll, to Inverary where he had once been held prisoner in the Tolbooth.

And now, all of the forces of the Greek tragedy began to move relentlessly forward toward death and destruction.

MacIain and his companions marched south. The next day, having struggled through the snow without stopping for warmth or sleep, they had only reached Loch Creran, less than half the way to Inverary, when the old man and his band were arrested by a party of Argyll's Regiment and were held in Barcaldine Castle for another twenty-four hours. When MacIain was released, it was the middle of the day of 1 January 1692. At dawn on 2 January, he arrived, exhausted by his ordeal, at Inverary. The sheriff, Campbell of Ardkinglas, was away, and it was not until 5 January that he returned. MacIain presented himself to take the oath. At first, he was refused, but then Ardkinglas relented and with great ceremony on the following day a humbled Alasdair

MacDonald of Glencoe, MacIain, signed the despised oath. However, the web of tragedy knitted tighter: the King and his council
must be consulted, since the MacDonald of Glencoe was five days
late, time had expired. And so, shortly after MacIain had made
his way back to his glen, the clerks of the Council in Edinburgh,
several of them Campbells, struck the name of Alasdair Mac-
Donald from the list of chiefs who had submitted to King and
Crown.

On 16 January, the King's order was sent out. The MacDonalds
of Glencoe were to be put to fire and sword. Secrecy, hatred and
greed all entered into a plot that began long before old MacIain
ever set out from Glencoe toward Fort William to the north and
Inverary to the south. There was now no turning back.

And so it was that on 1 February, the unwritten law of the
Highlands was evoked: strangers, travellers, two companies of
Argyll's troops plus some of Drummond's grenadiers, asked for
hospitality and, true to tradition, they were received by MacIain
and were sheltered by MacDonalds up and down the valley. For
twelve days they were guests of the clan and treated as friends, for
that was the law. On the stormy morning of 13 February, at five
o'clock, the law was broken. Those who had been sheltered and
fed by their hosts, at the orders of their chief murdered without
mercy, men, women and children. Some fled, up into the high
passes, only to die in the blizzard; some escaped and lived to tell
the story. The King washed his hands like Pilate and indicated
that his orders had been carried out much too rigorously. But no
one was punished. And therein lies the mystery.

Glencoe, after the massacre, was a deadly quiet little valley,
smoke from the burning cottages mingling with the heavily fal-
ling snow, blood lying in small pools around the bodies that were
soon to be laid to rest decently on the Isle of St Munda in Loch
Leven, the burial place of the MacDonalds of Glencoe.

Glencoe, today, is still an awesome little valley. There are some
who say that Glencoe should best be seen, to be fully appreciated,
on a dismal day of rain and fog. Frankly, although I suppose it
does, I cannot imagine the sun ever shining sweetly on Glencoe,
once called an enclosed garden. I doubt whether I would ever feel
happy in that valley, even on the loveliest of summer days. I don't
need rain or sun in Glencoe, the place where the time-honoured

law of the Highlands was broken. For me, the valley will always be a place of horror. For me, it will always be snowing there, and the air acrid with smoke. When I am there, in that valley of tears, I shiver and see things I ought not to see. Legend has it that the people of Glencoe were born with the second sight. Though not of Glencoe, I too was born with the second sight – a mixed blessing, to be sure, especially when one's vision is capable of casting one backwards into a history best forgotten.

The massacre at Glencoe should be forgotten. I have recounted it so that the tourist may know what happened there and show respect to the helpless victims, the women and the children. It was a dastardly deed, not a page in Scotland's history to be dwelt upon. There was no chivalry, nothing in which to take pride, only cruelty, treachery and greed. If we want to think about Scottish history, let us turn our thoughts to Bannockburn and Stirling Bridge, to Wallace and Robert the Bruce and Prince Charles Edward, to St Margaret and the Fair Maid of Perth, to the sacred Isle of Iona and Scone where kings were crowned, to Andrew Carnegie and James Watt. Such is the glory of Scotland.

27. The Revenge

'I KNOW what they are,' said Freddie with some asperity one night at dinner. 'They're Mussolini's revenge.'

'Who are what?' I asked, looking up from the *pâté*.

'The Italian waiters. They're Mussolini's revenge on the British for winning the war.'

He had hit the nail right on the head. This remark was made some time ago, and year after year we've seen no change in the lamentable situation. But we still cherish hopes.

For some odd reason, economics or a misguided idea of cachet, the management of large British hotels recruit waiters, head-waiters and *maîtres-d'hôtel* from Italy. Perhaps that is what they think foreign visitors want: suave waiters, urbane, with a Continental flourish. The devil they are! They're churlish and sneering and they make the paying guests feel that a very big favour is being done them when they deign to take their orders.

They also tend to look down their noses when a *table d'hôte* dinner is ordered instead of more expensive *à la carte* choices. Except for a few, notable and nice exceptions, they are gaining a bad reputation for Scottish hotels and we would love to see them all packed off to Italy and let them insult guests where insults are expected.

The sort of treatment lavishly doled out by the Italians is totally un-Scottish and it would be far, far better were the managers to fire them and put in their places young Scots who need the work and who are polite to visitors to their country.

Until that happy day, the victimized tourist has only one recourse. Fight back, but *quietly.* You're paying the bill, remember. At the first lifted eye-brow or disdainful curled lip, stare coldly. If this fails to penetrate, take a positive stand the next time you are served a helping of rudeness. Don't shout at the waiter that you are going to report him to the manager of the hotel. Just state, in a quiet voice in English that he can understand, that if this treatment continues, you will feel it your *duty* to report him. Hopefully, you will see a distinct change in his attitude: as you enter the dining room, the peasants (alias the other guests) will be swept out of your way and you will be wafted on a golden cloud of reverence to your table, especially if it was the *maître-d'hôtel* you have just ticked-off. You may find that your reserved table, back in a corner behind a pillar or beside the kitchen swinging doors, has been moved front and centre. Italians are fearful snobs.

A word to the wise (or un-wise): do remember that you are in a country where good manners and a soft voice, even when you may be tried to the absolute length of your endurance, count far more than money or position. Don't be critical of the food or service in general. Criticism for the sake of criticism alone is a lost art in Scotland, I am happy to say, and the Scots don't need any visitors making waves in their placid life stream. Not that the Scots, themselves, are incapable of making a row. On the contrary. But when firing a rocket, just don't use dynamite. Modulation, that's the answer!

The hierarchy of a resort hotel's dining room aristocracy is very strange indeed, and quite unfair to Scotland. The top echelon in the main are those Italians; a select few of the waiters are miraculously Scottish; and the labouring *commis* in their toe-touching white aprons are generally Scottish, but utterly intimidated by the Italians. Sometimes, I feel like organizing a strike, but Freddie always tells me to calm down, it's not my problem. Yes, but there's a *principle* involved!

Thank Heaven, this is not true of *all* Scottish hotels. The situation is only found in the large, lush establishments. However, in some of these hotels, I really must admit in all truth, the majority of the waiters may be Scots – an oversight, no doubt, on the part of the management. And then each meal is pure delight if you're lucky enough to draw a Scottish waitress. She'll coddle you and cosset you and you'll eat far too much for your own good and she'll beam with pleasure as she urges 'just a wee bittie more' on you. *This* is true Scottish hospitality!

Many other Continental Europeans work in the big hotels and, with a few reservations, you'll have no problem with them. You'll find some very nice young German waiters, often students on holiday. The floor maids and the barmen, if not Scots, are often Spanish, and they know the true meaning of service without being servile. The ones on which to keep an eagle-eye are the French housekeepers and the Irish waitresses who look like prize-fighters in disguise. They were born with chips trembling on their shoulders. You just have to take them in your stride.

But, beware of Mussolini's Revenge!

28. The Glorious Twelfth

I'VE HEARD more than one of my English friends refer to the Scots as 'barbarians, y'know'! A purely personal expression, granted, but one that manages to raise my hackles alarmingly. The mere mention to the English that one would choose to go to Scotland to *live* affects them very much as would a smack in the face with a wet mackerel. There *are* those Londoners who refer to Scotland as 'God's Country' – and they're right – but in the main the Southerner's or Sassenach's opinion is that Scotland is a bleak, mountainous land peopled by a totally uncivilized mob that not so long ago skulked about purloining each other's livestock. According to them, this does not, of course, decidedly not, apply to those Anglicized 'county' Scots who went south to school and university,

speak pure Oxbridge and keep large establishments in the country 'up there'. Where the English draw the line, I'm never quite
certain. A Scot is a Scot no matter where he went to school, or how
he speaks, or who he entertains; and upon certain occasions his
very Scottishness will show like a well-starched petticoat, or a stiff
lace jabot. After all, who but a Scot would go about in this day and
age with lace at neck and wrists without so much as a quiver of
embarrassment?

However, there is one day when every Englishman of position
and means will crawl, if no other means of transport is possible,
north, to the northern counties of England and *even,* and chiefly,
to Scotland. In England's social calendar, August the twelfth is
the time to be in Scotland. Suddenly, it is quite all right; in fact,
'the thing to do'.

August the twelfth is 'The Glorious Twelfth'. Now, this is likely
to mean nothing at all to the average visitor, except that it sounds
a bit like the American 'Glorious Fourth'.

All of this social hullabaloo is caused by the *Lagopus Scoticus,* a
very small wild bird otherwise known as the red grouse. And why
all of the excitement? Because on the twelfth day of August you
can lawfully shoot the poor little devil, that's why. This day marks
the beginning of the grouse season. In September, the 'civilized'
mob point their guns and shooting sticks in a northerly direction
and commence decimating the pheasant population. On August
the twelfth the 'season' opens in Scotland. Country houses,
shooting lodges and hotels positively swarm with men in tweeds
and stout boots, stamping about at dawn, clambering into shooting brakes and being driven pell-mell off into those hilly moor-
lands that at other times they call 'desolate'.

This is not a poor man's sport, for shooting over another man's
land for wild birds is a very expensive business. A moor inhabited
by grouse can be a sound economic investment, and I've seen
many a parcel of property advertised for sale with a number of
acres of grouse moor and the number of grouse killed neatly
tabulated year by year.

I like grouse, beautifully roasted, with a bit of bacon on its tiny
breast, with fried breadcrumbs on the outside and bits of buck-
shot on the inside, as well as anyone. Therefore, I suppose it is
unpardonably hypocritical of Freddie and me to dash about the

countryside prior to August the twelfth shouting to any *Lagopus Scoticus* intelligent enough to understand, like Paul Revere: 'The English are coming! The English are coming!' Perhaps there *is* a real similarity between 'The Glorious Twelfth' and 'The Glorious Fourth'.

29. *Where Ossian Lies*

ALL too often a visitor's time in Scotland is limited, so that a trip up into the Highlands is impossible. In such a small country this does sound rather strange, but the great mountains lie well to the north of the Glasgow–Edinburgh area, and because the country is ribbed like an old washboard, the roads can't always go in a straight line. This is unfortunately true in the Grampians and the North-western Highlands, where roads must follow glens which do not always go in the direction you feel you ought to be going, or they wind up and around and down and up again in tortuous tracks. This is all very time consuming. Not that one wants to get out on the roads and race from A to Z, because what lies *between* A and Z is why you're going to Z in the first place. In Scotland, it's not that Z has any special charms; it's just that Z is where you plan to spend the night.

If that sounds complicated, it simply means that your destination is generally not as important as the ground over which you travel. This is a difficult fact for Americans to digest, but it's terribly important to adjust to it in Scotland, where the pace, thank goodness, is not that of the New World. Besides, in the Highlands there's really nothing to see except the scenery, which is why you're up there in the first place. So don't rush. Stop at the lay-bys and look at the vast sweep of grey-blue peaks ranging outward as far as the spell-bound eye can see. Or just get out of the car and deeply breathe in the mountain air or pick some heather. One doesn't hurry in the Highlands. It's just plain dangerous on the single lane roads, especially, where driving can be tricky. Then, there's the traffic. During the summer months, the roads are crawling with trailer/caravans, motor bikes, land-rovers piled with camping equipment, and cars full of tourists completely indoctrinated in the race-course philosophy, to say nothing of the buses and trucks. Besides, you will probably still not be used to 'this wrong side of the road' driving as you will persist in calling it. So, take it easy.

Thus, I say, if you can't spend three or four days up in the Highlands, poking about with no Estimated Time of Arrival anywhere that *really* matters, may I suggest that you consider a substitute plan?

If you are in Edinburgh or Glasgow, there's a lovely day's drive you can take that will show you the very essence of the Highlands. No, I don't mean driving along the west shore of Loch Lomond, which is like so many resort lakes in the United States, or up into the Trossachs which are like resort hills in the United States. These are not what you came to Scotland to see. I'm not prejudiced against Loch Lomond: it's just that the traffic is always so fierce that you can't enjoy the scenery. As to the Trossachs, at the risk of being very unpopular, I admit that I *am* against them. They're baldish, uninteresting in some spots, and over-manicured in others. The real Highlands have not been groomed, decorated with craft shops and studded with pipers standing forlornly in dusty trampled heather. The Highlands do not look like a stage setting for a second-rate *Lucia di Lammermoor*. Besides, the Lammermuir Hills are south-east of Edinburgh, and they are charming. The Highlands are wild sometimes, depressing occasionally, and most often exhilarating. One feels the Highlands deep in one's bones and spirit. Once you're in them you become part of them. These mountains are not something you can regard objectively: they won't let you.

So, if you have a car, drive from either Glasgow via Stirling and the Castle, or from Edinburgh across the Forth Road bridge up into Perthshire to the town of Crieff that overlooks the lovely valley of the River Earn, 'Bonnie Strathearn'. From there drive a few miles east on the Perth Road and you will arrive at a small settlement called Gilmerton. Make a sharp left turn up the road marked to Amulree, Glen Almond and Aberfeldy (822). This is the road that takes you through 'The Sma' Glen' which is the Highlands in microcosm. Here you are more or less alone, give or take a few cars and a good deal of sheep. To us, this is one of the loveliest drives in all Scotland, and year after year we never tire of it. In some spots it is rugged, the road spiralling up past a waterfall wreathed with heather clinging precariously to the rocks. In the glen itself the steep mountain sides drop down sheerly, almost to the sides of the road. Beyond the glen is a wild moor which in the season is covered with sportsmen banging away at the wild birds. It is in the Sma' Glen that Ossian, the ancient poet, is supposed to be buried – not that it is going to unduly excite many people, including myself.

Beyond Amulree, now out of the glen, you have a choice of routes. You may turn east to Dunkeld and thence to the road to Perth (9), which will take you to Birnam wood of *Macbeth* [*sic*] which never did, as you can see, come to Dunsinane. From Perth, the major highway will whisk you easily back to Edinburgh. If this is not your choice, you might want to continue on to Aberfeldy, an equally lovely drive down to the River Tay. On either road, to Aberfeldy or to Dunkeld, you will catch glimpses of the hunting lodges of some very wealthy people, and streams and burns rushing down to join the Tay, where fishermen stand hip-deep in the icy, swirling water.

From Aberfeldy back to the city you may go a variety of different ways: along Loch Tay (827) to Killin and Callander (85), or to Lochearnhead and Comrie. Both Tay and Loch Earn are beautiful, especially on a clear day when the opposite shore is reflected in the mirror quiet waters of the loch and water rushes in silver spates down the sides of the mountains, eventually to feed the hungry sea.

30. *The Drawn Blind*

THERE IS one lamentable facet to tourism in Scotland, not from the Scots' point of view, but for the visitor bent upon shopping for goodies to take home.

This is an occurrence, or lack of it, called 'Early Closing', and it can have a frustrating effect upon unwitting shoppers. There is nothing worse to the diligent shopper, bent upon picking up a tweed skirt or a new set of golf clubs, than to find the shop closed and bolted.

To make matters even worse, the various towns and cities do not all observe the same early closing days. For instance, Peebles –

where you might want to purchase a pullover, a cardigan or a twin-set – is closed for the afternoon on Wednesday. If you yearn for golf clubs from St Andrews, don't try to get them there on Thursday afternoon. Perth, an excellent shopping centre, also closes on Wednesday afternoon, so buy your River Tay pearls in the morning or on some other day. To make things even more interesting, some towns, especially resorts or tourist centres, don't close during the 'season'. But how do you know if you're in 'season' or not?

In Edinburgh, the fishmongers close on Monday (not that you're pining away for fish), the drapers and jewellery stores close on Tuesday (here you could be disappointed) and on Wednesday it's chaos, for then you are denied by bakers, butchers, grocers, drugstores (except for medications), hairdressers and stationers. However, the shops on Princes Street, and those that cater for the tourists' business stay open all week until one o'clock on Saturday. After all, they have to escape from frantic shoppers sometime!

Frankly, I have no idea whether the tourist shops stay open as they do in Edinburgh, but in Glasgow the early closing days are Tuesday *and* Saturday.

To be absolutely certain, check with your hotel hall-porter, or consult a city guide or your tourist guide book. But, remember, rules are made to be changed: 'Britannia waives the rules.'

31. Anyone for Ghosts?

TELL A Scotsman that he's superstitious and he'll probably take umbrage. He'll doubtless inform you that you're being *ridiculous*! And that out of *his* mouth can be a real crusher.

But he is, you know.

In Edinburgh on the night of 18 August 1513, a sepulchral voice issued from the Mercat Cross in the deep shadow of the High Kirk of St Giles. The voice, from beyond reality, read in awesome tones the names of those who would die in the proposed battle between the Scots and the forces of Henry VIII. Among the names on that eerie roll-call was that of the King, James IV, as well as those of many of his nobles. In spite of the entreaties of James' queen, Margaret Tudor, sister of Henry, the King pursued his plan to do battle against the English in order to weaken Henry's army, who was also fighting the French in Flanders. This was in the cause of the Auld Alliance and it seemed that every time the Scots had any dealings in their alliance with the French, the Scots lost more than they gained. At four o'clock on the afternoon of 9 September, James entered into ill-advised battle at Flodden Field, just over the border in England, on the banks of the River Till. When it was over, there lay dead upon the field James IV, one of his illegitimate sons, an archbishop, a bishop, earls, clan chiefs, lairds and gentlemen, in addition to his regular fighting men from hill and glen and lowland farms. In all, ten thousand men died. Although I tend to doubt that the supernatural voice of the Mercat Cross read out all ten thousand names, it did foretell the future with ghastly accuracy. The very flower of Scotland lay dead on Flodden Field, and few homes throughout the land were not touched by loss and grief.

> The Flowers of the Forest, that foucht aye the foremost –
> The prime o' our land – are cauld in the clay.

For many years, the tune that accompanies these verses of the Jane Elliot version of 'The Flowers of the Forest' which I have quoted only in brief, has been the lament played on the bagpipes in honour of Scottish dead.

Centuries have passed, but the roll-call of the dead by the unearthly voice on an August night has been remembered by the Scots. The voice spoke, the battle occurred and the King and his loyal supporters did die. These things cannot be glibly explained away.

Is it any wonder, then, that the Scots are superstitious? They are imbued with a belief in the supernatural, in ghosts, fairies, goblins, visions, the magical flag of the MacLeods; and above all, many have 'the second sight'.

The majority of Scots are Celts or a mixture thereof and thus, they are fertile ground for the seeds of superstition. The word 'superstition' may be offensive to some people because it implies a foolish, illiterate and gullible quality. *This* the Scots do *not* possess. Superstition has several meanings, chiefly a blindly accepted belief, regardless of reason, in a circumstance or occurrence, often ominous. However, the Scots do believe in the unseen. Many of them boast of it, many grudgingly admit it, and many say it is all so much 'stumpish blether'. It is the latter who will, even so, avoid cemeteries at night and warn their children away from the 'hantit hoosie'.

Out of Highland folklore and tales of the hyperphysical have come such legends as *Tir-nan-Og* – the Land of the Young, a never-never-land where fairies live in hills and on islands. There is the story of the living toad found in the black heart of a hollow stone, and another of the phantom hunt that has been heard in the far north, the voices of the unseen hunters and hounds raised in full cry. There is widespread belief in the Loch Ness monster. There is also belief in the Loch Morar monster, whose appearance is said to foretell a death in the family of MacDonnell of Morar. The Fergussons of Glenshellish have their own monster of impending doom, a bat with a human face, the *brideag,* which appears at a window as an ominous omen.

Witches, from high station and low, were once common and many were burned at the stake for using spells and enchantments. One of very high degree was the sixteenth century Joan Douglas, Lady Glamis, an ancestress of H.M. Queen Elizabeth, the Queen Mother. However, Lady Glamis was executed by fire not because she was a witch – which she was not – but for motives of revenge. The accusation of using the black arts was often a convenient way to get rid of inconvenient enemies.

At St Fillans, in Perthshire, is a healing well where those devoted to the saint could drink and bathe in the waters and cures were devoutly recorded, supposedly to the glory of the saint.

Ghosts abound in Scottish castles, and they are a rather peculiar bunch. Ireland has her share of ghosts, too, but they are generally of the pitiful breed, more often hideously malevolent. Scottish ghosts tend to be a cheery lot, with a sense of humour, and they seem to feel a need for human companionship. If this sounds as though I believe in ghosts, I do.

An old friend of mine, now deceased, a soldier and a most erudite gentleman and chieftain, claimed to possess two in his castle and he offered to introduce me to them, or them to me, which I suppose would be the more correct protocol, since they quite obviously have the upper hand. I'd not like to have got off

G 2

on the wrong foot – there's nothing more pesky than a miffed ghost. My friend had never seen them during his lifetime, but as I have the second sight it was hoped that the pleasure would be mine. He assured me that both ladies (since it may be assumed that *they* are still there), are supposed to be of a kindly nature. I do like nice-mannered ghosts, for I was once kicked by a ghost in America, which I thought was most uncivilized and rather typical of the 'colonies'. It turned out that this Virginia ghost was a woman: which brings up a point of interest: ghosts usually seem to be women. Is it because women are always reputed to have the last word?

Scottish clans have long histories that twist and turn back into the murk of time. Each clan in the old days had its bard, and before clan gatherings he had to prepare himself to record vocally, without cue cards, the heroic, superhuman, legendary exploits of the clansmen, especially the chiefs and chieftains, back to the year dot.

Is it any wonder, then, that these people believed, and perhaps still do, in portents of evil and good, of moon-struck persons, of huge black cats, of goblins in the hills and evil trout in the streams and rivers? The latter belief, by the way, is *not* limited to frustrated fishermen.

Second sight is relatively common, and those who have it don't hide their light under a bushel. My grandmother possessed it, as I do myself. It is not at all frightening, and sometimes I am quite grateful because it has cushioned me for shocks and other unexpected events. Mine is rather personal and is limited to myself and my family, though only the Brahan Seer knows how it might develop in my old age. Since my flashes of insight are swift and difficult to articulate at the time, Freddie tends to discount my faculty, which I suppose is natural for one who has never had the experience himself. He has not proposed that quiet place in the country with iron bars on the casements as yet, but to calm his fears, I really must nail down one of my better, happier 'sights' some day and tell him about it in advance of the future event. *Posto facto* is a bit too *ad hoc*. For Freddie and for most men, it is pure *post hoc ergo propter hoc* which is just another way of saying, 'woman's illogical reasoning'.

A Lowland Scot may try to tell you that only Highlanders are superstitious. If that is so, why was there a fairy boy of Leith, which is the port of Edinburgh, and why are so many prose accounts and poems concerning the supernatural written in Lallans, the language of the Lowlander? What about Burns' 'Tam O'Shanter', the Ayrshire man who saw an 'unco sight'? Remember his 'warlocks and witches in a dance' and 'Auld Nick, in shape o' beast' playing the pipes?

No, deny it as they may, superstition and the supernatural are part of the Scottish national fabric. After all, there's nothing wrong with it – so long as it doesn't interfere with business!

An obvious answer that springs to many people's lips is that all this is past history. They forget about the woman in the South Orkneys who dreamed one night of a blonde lady with golden earrings lying dead on a rock above the sea – and the next day came the news of the wreck of a steamer, only a few miles from the woman's cottage, with the loss of thirty-six lives. One of the drowned was a fair-haired lady wearing gold earrings who was found on the rocks where the sea had flung her body. This was in 1937 – not such very past history.

Last of all, there's Hogmanay (New Year's Eve), celebrated all over Scotland, when each family hopes that the first person to cross their thresholds after midnight will be a dark-haired man, bearing three gifts: whisky, a lump or two of coal, and salt or bread or cakes, tokens to insure the household food, warmth, prosperity and long life. Last Hogmanay, two young Scotsmen dropped by our house, separately. The first carried no 'handsels', as he came before midnight and had red hair, so he knew he would bring no luck to the house. The second came just after twelve o'clock. His hair is dark and he handed me gifts of buns, matches, an evergreen bough and a bottle of whisky. He hadn't a doubt in his mind that he brought good fortune with him. Both these men are scientists, one a doctor of medicine, the other a physicist. But were I to tell them that they were superstitious, they would both impale me with an awful stare and snort 'Ridiculous!'

32. People Seated All About

THE LOUNGE is the nerve centre of Scottish hotels, especially in the country where the guests are held more or less captive in the evening simply because there's nowhere else to go. In the cities, especially in Edinburgh during Festival time, it's a different matter: but an hour or two spent in the lounge can be a reasonably entertaining way to fill the yawning gap between dinner and bedtime.

Hotels in Scotland fall, roughly, into three categories.

The first is the *de luxe*, terribly pukka establishment in the resort areas. The second, the hotels in the cities and towns that cater mostly for foreign visitors and the third are country hotels in the same regions as the first, but not as pretentious. I am not including the family-type hotels, or the bed-and-breakfast tourist homes that abound in Scotland.

The evening spent in the lounge has long been a British tradition, and in consequence, therefore, all sorts of unwritten rules have become as firmly entrenched as some of the long-term guests. No matter what role the lounge plays during the day – waiting-room, tea-room or card-room – at night it becomes ballroom and drawing room. That is where one takes after-dinner coffee, dances if there *is* dancing, and watches the other guests. It is not a conversation pit except under certain circumstances.

The procedure at a Scottish resort hotel in the evening is as stately as a strathspey and no more flexible in its pattern. First, you descend from your room, dressed appropriately to the type of hotel, at approximately seven to seven-thirty. Dress is well-defined. For the men, black tie if the hotel is 'that kind', or business or lounge suit if it is not. Leave the blazer or sports jacket in the wardrobe. The ladies should bring one long dinner dress if they are going to a resort hotel, for the British love to dress up in the evening, like children in a masquerade, and the same dress may be worn night after night if its wearer can stand it. The hotel and its guests couldn't care less. I know an elderly English lady visitor who has worn the same dinner dress every night, season after season. And why not? It's black and it's lace and it cost a fortune. Dressing on Friday and Saturday nights is *comme il faut,* and strictly so, but Sunday night is 'let-down' night and no one dresses. (By that I mean one would dress as for a cocktail party at home – the British never let down *too* far!) You understand, though, that this is for the resorts only.

Once downstairs, one naturally gravitates to the bar. As opposed to the United States, there is no long cocktail hour (often a misnomer for 'hours') before dinner. The British like a drink or two merely as a warm-up for dinner, *not* as a substitute. In fact, should you ever be invited to a British home for dinner and the card or note reads 'seven-thirty for eight o'clock', this means in translation that you arrive *promptly* at seven-thirty, drink for half an hour, and have dinner served punctually at eight o'clock. If you arrive ten minutes before eight o'clock, you've just about lost your drinking time because dinner will be served at the announced hour. But, if drink means that much to you, don't worry. Wine will be served at table, and there will be plenty of time to drink afterwards. The British believe in first things first – like dinner for example.

So I suggest a relaxing thirty to forty-five minutes in the bar. Here one's good manners as a visitor can be demonstrated. In most bars the chairs are grouped about tiny tables, like a living room, and that is how it should be treated. If you are only two, find a pair of chairs: please don't take over a large grouping in the corner just because you are early and the place is at the moment vacant. There will be large parties coming in later and courtesy dictates that you use only as much space as you really need. The British would never be so thoughtless as to hog a huge grouping while a party of six or eight cast about helplessly for places to sit. It just isn't done!

I have been referring to the guests as British, even though I am talking about Scottish hotels, for a simple reason: most of the well-heeled residents are English up for the season, or passing through on their way to the country places of friends. The rest are foreigners – Americans, Spanish, Italian, French or German. There are a *few* Scots, but not many. This type of resort caters mostly for the English carriage trade, but I don't like to use the words 'English courtesy' when the Scots' courtesy is just as good, if not better. They can't be penalized by giving the lion's share of

praise to the English, simply because the Scots aren't fully and
equally represented. It's a fine point, but I'm certain you'll see
what I'm driving at.

After a leisurely dinner, you stroll into the lounge. It should by
now be about ten o'clock. This is where the subtle fun comes in, if
you go for such parlour games, as I hope you do. If it is your first,
or only evening, in the hotel, let the waiter or waitress seat you, for
were you to choose your own spot you might break one of those
unwritten rules of the lounge. While the British are flexibly polite
when it comes to places in the bar, their squatters' rights in the
lounge after dinner are inalienable. Best let waiter or waitress be
your guide: they know who has sat where since time immemorial.
Sir A. and Lady B. must sit in the chairs closest to the band
because Sir A. is somewhat deaf. My lord has listened to my lady
all during dinner and he needs a musical interlude. Colonel C.,
C.B.E., D.S.O., M.C., and his elderly shooting companion want
their seasonal chairs as far away from the band as possible so they
can rumble on about the 14-18 (World War 1 to you) and, yet,
close enough to the dance floor so they can ogle the girls up from
London. Lady D., whose deceased spouse was merely a knight,
feels most at ease if she and her restive teen-age granddaughter
sit in a far, dim corner, because she knows that the money and the
knighthood came from the manufacture of sausages, a humiliation not assuaged by the undoubted superiority of the product.
Mrs. E and her wispy companion must sit by the gas logs in the
fireplace, under a floor lamp with a pink silk shade where the light
is best for her knitting and her companion's needlepoint. A Canadian millionaire and his wife have for years been ensconced on a
sofa just inside the doors, a vantage point for observation and
muttered commentary. And that's the way it goes, and were you
to take their places you would incur hostile glares. This is not a
criticism of their good manners, but yours.

At last, safely and respectfully seated, you are brought coffee
and you may sit back in your arm chair and watch the goings-on.
First, there is the ballroom dancing. The women, on the whole are
fairly skilled, but Englishmen have never been known for their
sense of rhythm when pitted against a group of musicians, Fred
Astaire being as notable an exception as the male dancers of the
Royal Ballet. At some point, especially on a Saturday night, a

piper will appear and reluctant groups will form jagged sets for a bit of touch-and-go Scottish dancing, just for 'good fellowship and no hard feelin's, don't y'know'. If you don't do Scottish Country Dancing, stay put. Even if you do square dancing at home, stay put. It's not the same thing at all as far as the feet are involved. These 'Mayfair Highlanders' are going to make a bonny enough sauce of it without your joining in. In fact, the whole drill is going to give you a very erroneous impression of this demanding and beautiful form of dancing. There may be one or two Scots in the group, and if the English will allow them the lead and 'cue on them' there may be a visible improvement. If you do know the dancing, take your place quietly and don't try to direct traffic. The English are experts at this themselves, even if they do finish by crashing into each other. The best thing you can do is to make certain that you know the dance, and dance it as well as you can. It's going to be the 'Eightsome Reel' anyway. You may politely unmuddle a reel that has gone awry, but don't issue any verbal orders. A gentle push in the right direction to avoid collision in 4/4 time will hardly be noticed in the mêlée that is going on around you.

The remainder of the evening is for more ballroom dancing, discreetly observing the comings and goings, and finally ordering a night-cap. You never know what you might see in this cosmopolitan array and, believe me, some of the sights will make you order another night-cap. In spite of your good intentions of early-to-bed, you may stay until the bitter end, long after Lady D. has betrayed her origins by ordering a nice 'cuppa' (tea, of course) before retiring. Round about midnight the usually sedate lounge takes on the quality of *Grand Hotel,* but that is the fault of a few footloose Americans coming in contact with some just plain loose Continentals, to the horror of the night porter, who by now has begun to pace back and forth like a turn-key in front of the glass doors.

As to the lounge not being a 'conversation pit', this is quite true. Some of the old, time-honoured guests who have known each other for years or even decades may have a quiet, reserved word in passing or they may even throw caution to the winds and draw up chairs and have a drink together. But, all in all, the whole performance has a Noah's Ark quality, each species carefully quarantined, with no attempt at social intercourse.

The second category of hotel lounges, those in the cities, are quite different. There one finds no music for dancing, at least as far as the lounge is concerned. The guests are either Scots businessmen staying the night on their way home from London, content to sip their coffee in silence while they digest the financial pages and their dinners. The rest of the migratory flock are foreigners. The Americans watch the Europeans and the Europeans watch the Americans. It is the rare and sophisticated American tourist who will study his fellow Americans. This pastime is short-lived, for at some point early in the evening the tour guide, European or American, dashes in breathlessly to summon his charges into a huddle to map out the next day's strategy and check synchronization of watches.

In the third classification, the country hotels of no affected pretensions, you find more relaxation and possible camaraderie. The latter will never reach the point of party spirit or friends for life, if the guests are English, but they may condescend at least to speak to you, and you may find a common ground for a brief conversation that will hurdle national reservations if you both are interested in 'huntin', fishin' or golfin' '. If the Englishman is tweedy, possibly retired from the forces, or a Chartered Accountant from Leeds, he might turn out to be rather jolly, and the next evening inquire as to successes back home in field and stream. If they are travelling with their wives, which is unlikely, the American wife may expect a hand-shake and a 'How d'y do' and a hand-shake and a 'good night' and little stimulation in between.

But, here are the places where you will encounter Scots on holiday, from Edinburgh or Glasgow, and this is quite a different matter. Not only will the Scots *speak*, they'll recognize you as Americans, buy you a drink and settle down for a good chat about their relatives who migrated to Rochester or Toronto or California. Before you've said a hearty good-night at an unholy hour, you're drunk with fellowship, you've exchanged cards and have arranged a golf game for the following morning. Your new friend won't ask you to fish or shoot with him, simply because he's paid for the privilege rather dearly and the price is for him alone and no new cronies. However, he'll be terribly regretful on this account. As to the ladies, they'll have their heads together over pictures of children and grandchildren and a very voluble conversation about American kitchens and the advantages of central heating and double glazing. When you leave *them*, you'll go to bed with a glowingly warm feeling and a totally new revelation about the basic goodness of people, especially the Scots. You'll probably even exchange Christmas cards in due course.

33. *Three Weeks In Summer*

EACH YEAR, from the latter part of August through to the early part of September, the Edinburgh Festival takes a grip on the city. This sounds a good deal more gay than it really is, and after each year's Festival the Scots ponder and wonder if it's all worth while. A few years ago it was discovered that only 9 per cent of the tickets were purchased by foreign visitors, so at that rate the Festival can't be very international! For this reason, the Festival has a rather *pro tem* quality and it always comes as a surprise when the schedule of events for the next year is announced. While the pro-Festival people and the anti-Festival people discuss whether or not it makes economical sense to continue, I'd like to add my own contribution to the pother.

If the festival directors would like to see more foreigners, especially Americans and Canadians, attending the Festival they would do well to advance the date to 1 August and carry on until 1 September. American couples with children at home, families travelling together, schoolteachers, professors and businessmen must all be back home by Labour Day, which marks the end of summer vacation-time and the return to school. As it is, the Americans are lucky if they can catch even one day of the Festival if they have responsibilities at home to be met by a certain date. I'm surprised that the canny Scots haven't taken this fact into account and by acting upon it, raised that lowly 9 per cent to unprecedented heights.

The Edinburgh International Festival is far from being a rowdy Mardi Gras. It is, rather, a sedate and cultured gathering of some of the world's greatest performers plus a more spritely fringe of youthful experimental theatre. The Festival is divided into several parts: music, ballet, drama, opera, art and films.

Music and ballet comprise performances by some of the greatest orchestras and dancers in the world. Drama offers trial-runs of some soon-to-be-great plays. Art exhibits are held at the Scottish Royal Academy and the Scottish National Gallery of Modern Art. The Edinburgh Film Festival is older than any other film festival except for those held at Venice and Cannes. As many as two-hundred films have been entered in the yearly competition. The 'fringe groups' offerings run from yet-undiscovered genius down to absolute rubbish.

The highlight of the Festival for foreign visitors is the Edinburgh Military Tattoo, which is held at night on the Castle Esplanade. This great colourful spectacle is the only one of its kind in a world in which the pomp, circumstance and precision of military ceremonial is fast becoming unpopular. The tattoo is by no means war-mongering. It is not a representation of the glory of battle, but an imposing display of the trappings of glorious nationhood, of pride in the physical accomplishment and vigour of its youth, of the grandeur of the music of its military bands, and of a deep respect for ancient and worthy traditions.

A good seat in the stands, high above the city, facing the floodlit Castle with the massed bands of famous regiments marching as one man, with horses going through intricate paces, dancing, comedy and feats of physical strength and agility, plus much more, all combine to provide incomparable entertainment.

After the bands have ceased playing and the spectators have finished singing the last old familiar song, a hush settles over the mighty Castle and the crowd before it. Then, high up on the now darkened battlements, a lone piper is picked out by a spotlight and, there, seemingly floating in the space of history, he plays the final tune of glory in solitary splendour.

34. The Lovable Scot

THE Standard Edition of the Scot, the vision that initially springs to mind, is that of a sour, stingy, slightly drunken sort who, if male, wears a mosaic kilt and supports himself on a knobbly walking stick. This is straight off the music-hall stage and is so untrue as to be quite worthy of its ignorant or obviously prejudiced source.

Those three words, 'sour', 'stingy' and 'drunken', make a very good place to start a totally fair debunking of the much maligned personality of the Scotsman. First, when the Scot is called 'sour' what is really meant is 'dour' – stern and unyielding. Certainly, the English have for many centuries of battles and other nasty contretemps been able to discover this to be an outstanding characteristic of their former adversary. But, yes, there are many Scots who are dour – not sour – simply dour. Some of it is mere façade, but, I admit, it does exist. However, since I believe it implies a steadfast, honest devotion to convictions, I think it is rather commendable to be dour.

'Stingy' is the last word I would apply to a Scot. Neither is he 'cheese-paring', another phrase that is often slapped on him. A Scot is thrifty in his expenditures and shrewd in his business dealings, but hospitable and so generous that he would give a needy friend the shirt off his back. To refute this calumny, take Andrew Carnegie. Dunfermline-born, this hard-working Scot never forgot his native land or his adopted country and countless towns and universities both in Scotland and America have received munificent gifts of libraries and educational buildings from his bequests. The thriftiness of the Scots has helped them over some grimly rough times in history. They pay their debts, and they don't waste money on frippery or things they don't really need. I could quote a whole list of pithy Scots proverbs to prove this point, but the best of them seems to be 'What gaes in at the dure gaes oot at the lum' which means what comes in at the door eventually goes up the chimney in smoke or, in plainer language, 'Fools and their money are soon parted.' Scots are *nobody's* fools. Nevertheless, they are generous to their friends and many are the kind, small, but highly personal gifts we have received from Scottish friends. I said that a Scot will give a friend the shirt off his back – and one of ours gave Freddie the socks off his feet, a beautiful pair of diced kilt hose he had worn just once at a function given by her majesty in London. He will never know how much that pair of socks means to 'young Fred'.

As to all Scots being drunks, this is inane. While statistically vague, my reasoning runs something like this: half of the Scots are children and half of the adults are women, so the percentage is cut down right there. Now, as to that quarter, according to my deduction, of the population represented by the men, some Scots don't drink at all, some are purely social drinkers, and some do a magnificent job of knocking it back. But, I've seen a minimum of falling-down, drunken Scots or those who needed to lean on their canes or *cromachs* to remain up-right. Certainly, there *are* some, but doubtless they have their own dark reasons for their habits. Actually, it's not easy to get drunk in Scotland. One reason is that whisky served over there is only 70° proof, while most of that which they export, especially to America, is a thumping 86.8° proof. A second and most important reason is that the whisky in Scotland, where it is distilled and blended, is *very* expensive, more so than in the places to which it is exported. The reason: the high tax. Therefore, whisky is drunk to be appreciated, not to get intoxicated on – not at those prices! The drink of the working man or the man with the lean purse is ale, beer or lager. Actually, Burns, the national poet and alleged drunkard, was an ale drinker. What passed for whisky in his day would have eroded teeth, cauterized tonsils and dissolved stomach linings. Interestingly enough, the Scots have no proverbs that have to do with an excess of drinking, although they've got sayings about almost *everything* else!

There is one facet of the personality of the average Scot which might earn him a peculiar reputation, but I do not find it detrimental. He *is* stand-offish. Not in the English sense, however, but quite differently. The English are snobbish; the Scots are not. In fact, I'd like to use the English as a comparison on this point. The English, their eyes alight with dogmatic zeal, cannot resist telling you what they think you should know or do for your own good. They feel it is their moral obligation to shove their advice down your throat even if you choke on it. Now, the Scot will never offer advice if it is not absolutely necessary and, if indeed you really want his advice you have to lay a good deal of ground work before any Scot will open his mouth about another man's business. He believes in live and let live. They've got a saying about that, too. 'Ilka ane maun winnae on his ain cannas.' And another, 'The soutar's bairns are aye the warst shod.' Both mean it's best to mind your own business. Now if that's what you call being stand-offish, then I'm all for it!

To keep this character analysis balanced, I must refer to a side of the Scots' nature that can neither be denied nor praised. They are as stubborn as curly-horned rams meeting on a narrow mountain track. They will not give way – and they do carry it to ridiculous extremes. In fact, they are rather complacent about it. Many is the clan slogan that incorporates some synonym that means, when you get down to the real bones of the matter, just plain stubborn. 'Stand fast!', 'I remain unvanquished', 'I am fierce with the fierce', 'Touch not the cat without a glove', 'No one attacks me with impunity', 'Conquer or die', and 'Courage grows strong at a wound'. There are some real gems there! Now, steadfastness is a fine thing, but there comes a time when one ought to know when to give in. But, no, not the Scots! In fact, they go so far as to remain stubborn *after* the very reason or need for it has disappeared. Then, they end by becoming angry, not with their protagonists, but, amazingly, with themselves, and the anger is followed by an awesome moodiness. As I have often said, the Scots are their own worst enemies. After all, it is rather short-sighted to be stubborn with oneself. It's such a waste of time that I wonder why these people, so chary of wasting anything, fall victims to such nonsense. But, there it is and there's nothing to be done about it. They themselves acknowledge this unfortunate trait when they say, 'He that wull tae Cupar, maun tae Cupar' – he who insists upon going to Cupar will *go* to Cupar. Don't worry about Cupar. It's in Fife. Coupar is in Angus. What they mean is that an obstinate person will do exactly as he pleases.

There are, however, several ways to combat this problem which will often meet with a certain amount of success. The first is to let him have his own way. This is not always popular, and not very good for the Scot. He feels invincible. The other is to make him think that what you want him to do, or not do, is his *own* idea. This is tricky, for Scots know when someone is cajoling them. They themselves are past-masters of the art of sophistry. But, if it is done subtly, then any problem or source of argument can be so easily solved that the Scot is then ready to do battle for something that he would have fought tooth-and-nail against before he was given 'The Treatment'. This is not a problem the tourist is likely to face, but it is a jolly good thing to know when a relative or friend is over-endowed with this far from endearing peculiarity.

Above all, only two things, as far as I can determine, matter to the Scots in their code of behaviour. All the rest is not worthy of their consideration. One is Pride, capital 'P', and Principle, ditto. Pride, to them, is not a cardinal sin, but a virtue. Principle is worth any amount of effort to uphold. These two characteristics have earned them quite a few nasty epithets from their critics – such as: stiff-necked, mulish, ruthless, unruly and swaggering, depending upon the source of the malediction. Nevertheless, if it weren't for the devotion to Pride and Principle and the willingnesss to die in support of these qualities the Scots would be a beaten, broken, poverty-stricken gaggle of people living in a dank, cold pocket of misery to the north of England.

Scots are clannish. They are happiest when they have their families around them. They may disagree among themselves, but woe betide any outsider who steps into the fray. Blood is thick, you know. They don't seem to have a proverb for that, but 'Bourdna wi bawtie' or 'Don't tease a large dog' will do as well as any and comes pretty close to the heart of the matter.

They are also quarrelsome, argumentative – not for the sake of the argument at hand, but for the sake of something *else* they may have gnawing at their minds, something quite different. This is further evidence of a devious trait that comes out in so many ways.

There you have it, the 'compleat Scotsman', stripped of his trappings of grandeur, peeled down to skin and muscle. He is not drunken, sour, stingy or inhospitable. He is obstinate, argumentative and, above all, moody, with violent depths and peaks, a veritable rollercoaster of emotions that might last ten minutes or ten years. He is also proud, honest and courageous. He is humorous, if you understand what he finds amusing and it doesn't happen to be your own frailties! And, he is obviously a great hand at turning out proverbs with indefatigable concentration.

Now, there is one thing I must make perfectly clear. Not all Scots *are* Scots, so many of these characteristics do not apply to them. Some Scots are really Irish, some Scots are really English, some are a mixture of both, or all, and others live on islands so far away from the mainland that they haven't received the word yet as to just how they should conduct themselves if they want to be considered Scottish.

There is no such thing as a 'professional Scotsman'. The 'professional Irishman' exaggerates his national characteristics. He is a burlesque of every trait that the world considers to be Irish. The Scot does not need to exaggerate himself or to be exaggerated by others. He already is more than life size. How could a caricature be made out of something so grandiose?

As I launched forth upon this discussion of Scottish temperament, I realized full well that I was skating, for personal and obvious reasons, on very thin ice, and that if the ice broke I should plunge through first. Anything that I say about the characteristics of the Scots applies to me, too, and it is difficult indeed to be objective. I feel like a psychoanalyst lying on his own couch, but 'physician heal thyself' to the contrary, it was good for me, I suppose. I'm just not altogether certain. I've been told that analysis lightens the psychological burden. That may well be true, but at the moment my psyche weighs a ton, and I wonder how I have put up with myself thus far in life. Worse, how does Freddie put up with me? Och, he isnae worth weel that winnae bide wae! Dinnae fash yoursel', Freddie, ye maun tak the ruch wi' the smooth.

35. Ye'll Aye Be Welcome Back

THE HIGH road, the low road. It matters not at all which road you travel. You may walk knee-deep in purple heather or thoughtfully re-trace the cobbled paths of history. A gentle rain may shroud in grey a loch, or the sun may shine, iridescent, on a distant glen. You may hear the song of the birds on a fresh country morning or the great voice of the pipes raised in wild exultation. A moment of sublime peace may await you in the cool, high mountains or on the sands beside the sea. Your road may take you to the Highlands or the Lowlands, but wherever the road leads it will bring you to a certain happiness, contentment and fulfilment that may only happen to you in that rare and magical land called Scotland, where a friend is 'yours aye'.